I0224093

You Are My Beloved

Messages From God

WILLIAM YELLES

DailyPossible
Los Angeles

Copyright © 2016 by William Yelles

All rights reserved. No part of this book may be used or reproduced in any manner whatsoever without written permission except in the case of brief quotations embodied in critical reviews or articles.

ISBN-13: 978-0692669129

No problem is too big for Me.
No prayer is too small for Me.
No wish is too impossible for Me.
GOD

CONTENTS

INTRODUCTION

The first day God spoke to me was Yom Kippur, the holiest on the Jewish calendar. But unlike the religious Jews dressed up fasting and praying to Him all day, I was soaking up the sun in shorts and flip-flops, devouring a maple-glazed donut — with bacon no less — contemplating what movie to see at the mall that afternoon.

Scrolling through showtimes on my phone, I began to feel a vague uneasy restlessness until it grew into a strong compulsion to head home and relax somehow.

A few years earlier, I may have chalked it up to guilt. But I had given up formal religious practice some time ago, and had no repressed desire to suddenly change into a suit and tie and hustle off to synagogue.

Once home, something inside me told me to pick up a pad of paper and pen, although I had no idea what for.

Describing the indescribable is an inexact science. The best way I can think of is that I started *feeling* words. It was as if they were appearing inside me from somewhere rather than I was consciously creating them myself. I started writing, or more like transcribing. At times it felt as if I could barely keep up with the pace of the flow.

Then just as quickly as it began, it was over. I found myself in an intense sweat, my heart racing, feeling incredibly discombobulated and light-headed. I would later discover it to be similar to how other people describe out-of-body experiences. My experience was definitely outside of time.

Thankfully God didn't pick up His cosmic Batphone to say He was mad at me. Or that my sins would not be forgiven like the ones in the fervent prayers He was hearing at that moment from around the world. Instead, I received a gift of pure love and joy so great that words can not fully express the supreme clarity and confidence with which I now move.

I've since experienced this same phenomenon dozens of times. These downloads alternate between God speaking to me in His own voice, with my own first-person (as if I'm a psalmist) or third-person. I have no real memory of receiving any of it. What happens during the dictation feels as if it happens in an instant yet each time hours pass and I've filled page after page of original, poetic, brilliant, direct Divine communication.

This book contains everything I've received to date, in exact order. Not a single word is altered. I inserted chapter and section breaks where the voice or theme changes to make it easier to read, and to open to any page and be inspired. Embrace the magic and mystery of finding the perfect words you need to read in a particular moment.

As you read this book, know these words do not come from me but through me.

Why me? For now, my answer is "Why not me?"

That may sound flip. But what I mean is God created all and is inside us all. Nothing is impossible. He is ready and able to have a conversation with anyone at any time, to provide guidance and hope, ecstasy and abundance, miracles and wonders beyond what we can conceive.

This is the God who you'll get to know in this book. The Great I Am, the same Presence who birthed trillions of stars and planets, and life itself.

GOD IS ALL THERE IS

No matter where I am, God is. I am clear, I am confident, I am led.

God is everywhere. God guides my every step.

God is All There Is. All good things come from God.

The devil is not real. It is distraction. It is a construct of the mind.

Fear is the work of the devil. Reality is communing with God.

In reality, we are all One. Nothing or no one can destroy us or distract us or depress us. The devil misleads. God is true.

We are all One in God even though each of us is unique.
We are different yet the same.

God is love. We are love.
God is great. We are great.
God is powerful. We are powerful.
God is creative. We are creative.
God is light. We are light.

God is All There Is. Nothing can stop God.

God is expressive. God expresses through you and me.

I am available for God to use me. I am right here. I am ready.

God holds the future. God holds the now.

God is confidence. We are confidence.

▪▪▪

The new begins in the invisible. Do not be afraid when you begin to see.

The new begins in the inaudible. Do not be afraid when you begin to hear.

The new begins when we sleep. Do not be afraid when you wake.

▪▪▪

I am a channel. I am a vessel.

God uses us as channels, as vessels of the all-good, of the all-is.

God is awake. I am awake. God is aware. I am aware.

God is real. God is all. We are One in God.

God is wonderful. I am wonderful. God is amazement. I am amazement.

God is beauty. God is love. I am beauty. I am love.

Divine love is a promise fulfilled. It begins as a whisper and becomes a roar.
It may sound like thunder yet it is calm like water. It flows.

Confusion is a construct of the mind.
God is never confused. God's path is clear.

My feet may stumble yet I walk in the land of the living.
My breath may grow weary yet God gives me strength.
My eyes may grow tired yet God helps me see.

Fear will perish. God never perishes.

When you feel something different than anything you ever felt before,
magic happens.

God shows up in the unexpected places, in the places never visited.
In the places never seen. In lands yet to be discovered.

God's secrets shine as the stars. God's power is greater than we can conceive. We have the power when we act as One.

▪▪▪

Where love is, God is. Where joy is, God is.
Where happiness reigns, God reigns.

God's goodness washes over us, making us clean.

When we are clear, we are aware. When we are awake, we are One.

Do not mistake this power as your own. It comes from God always, God Almighty, God All-Beauty, God in all space and time, in all things, in all there is, and yet to be born, in all there ever was and all there will ever be.

I do not know why. God has the answers to questions never asked.

God holds children in His arms who are yet to be born.
God holds our dreams. God holds our passions.

We must thank God for wishes fulfilled, for the miracles all around us.

God's work never ceases. Time may pass. God has not.

God is in the invisible, in the inaudible. God is always here, ever present, never changing, never ceasing to amaze.

God carries us when we are weak.

▪▪▪

These words are coming from another space. They are not coming from me, but through me. They are from another time.

I know there is an All-Knowing, a Presence that is here always.

God's wonders are beyond our comprehension. They can not be predicted, yet should be expected.

God is always here. He keeps us strong.
God always listens. He helps us hear.

When God is our strength, we are always strong.

When God is our courage, we are not afraid.

In times of confusion, God is not confused. He needs us as His vessels.

In times of challenge, God is unstoppable.
In times of fear, God is hope.
In times of trouble, God is our escape.

God shows up in unexpected people, places, and times. He never leaves us.

God is in control. We are not.

God gives us the drive to walk, yet He walks with us.
God gives us the courage to stand and He stands with us.

God gives us hearts to feel and mouths to speak.
God is in our love and in the words we say.

When life feels out of control, God is in control.
When time moves fast, God is eternal.
When time moves slow, God is never far away. He never leaves us.

The world is ever changing. God is not.

▪▪▪

"Help me have the courage to see," we ask, and God helps us see.

God is in the air we breathe, in the sun that shines, in the stars that soar.

God is in the everyday. God is in the ordinary yet God does the extraordinary.

God is here for us, yet He needs us. We need God so we may do His work.

God is greatness. We are greatness.
God gives us courage. We are courage.
God gives us hope. God is hope.
God gives us strength. He is our strength.
God never forsakes us. He is always here.

Beauty is ever present. God is ever present. Joy is eternal. God is eternal.

We marvel in the wonder that all is possible. God makes all things possible. Nothing is impossible for God unless we think it so.

God gives us strength because He needs our strength. Our strength shows up in the invisible spaces where God is.

God sees what we do not see. God hears what we do not hear.

When we cry, God wipes our tears.
When we sleep, God holds us.
When we walk, God moves us.
When we feel, God loves us.
When we do not feel, God loves us.
When we fail, God forgives us.

God's love is eternal. God is eternal.

God is All There Is.

■■■

When we are afraid, God keeps us safe.
God is our protector. He shields us from harm.

When we listen, God speaks. When we speak, God listens.

God always hears us when we do not hear.
God always sees us when we do not see.

God calms us when we are afraid.

When we are confused, God gives us clarity.
When we are anxious, God gives us peace.
When we are hopeless, God calms our minds.
When we are restless, God helps us rest.
When we are lost, God shows us the way.

While we are confused, God is clear.

He gives us the strength to carry on when we have no strength.

In the darkness of night, He is present.
When we call His name, He responds.

God shows us what is possible when we do not see.
God holds our hands when we need to feel.
God helps us stand when we are weary.
God gives us the courage to believe when we do not believe.
God believes in us when we do not believe in Him.
God gives us the answers before we ask the questions.
God gives us beauty when all we see is darkness.

God is in still waters and troubled waters.

God is the ocean of possibility. He will not let us drown.

We float on the wave of God.

KNOW THAT I AM HERE

Magic happens when we are open to it:

Be not afraid, I Am your strength.
Be not weary, I Am your courage.
Be not scornful, I Am your love.

I Am in your heart, in your mind, in your hands and feet.
I help you feel. I help you think. I help you touch. I help you walk.

When you cannot walk anymore, I will carry you.
When you are lonely, know that I Am always here with you.
When you feel, I feel. When you hurt, I hurt.

Your pain is My pain. Your joy is My joy. Your love is My love.

In your darkness, I Am your light.
In your confusion, I Am your clarity.
In times of trouble, I Am your rock, your salvation.

Know that I Am here when you do not see Me.
Know that you are My vessel even when you do not know why.

I Am The Answer to your question before you have asked.

I see when you do not see.
I believe when you do not believe.
I love when you do not love.

I give you courage when you are weak.
I calm your fears when you are afraid.

You are My channel. You are My vessel.
You are My child. I Am your Heavenly Father.
You are My pride. You are My joy.

▪▪▪

Humanity is My greatest creation. I've given you the capability to feel Me. I've given you the capacity to love. I've given you the chance and the courage to open your hearts and let Me in.

Where there is no door, I will make an opening.
Where there is no path, I will build a bridge.
Where there is no sun, I will light your way.

▪▪▪

Be open. Be available. Be not afraid.

I Am your courage. I Am your strength.
I Am your salvation from trouble.

I will calm your mind in times of confusion.
I will help you stand when you cannot walk.
I will help you speak when you do not know the words to say.

I will show you love in times of hate.
I will show you peace in times of war.
I will show you beauty in times of darkness.

I will give you joy when you are tired.
I will give you riches when you are poor.

I will show you the way. When there is no way, I will make a way.

When you have no fire, I will light a spark. My flame is eternal.

When you believe in Me, there is no darkness.
There is only light. There is no bad, only good.

When you speak, I listen. I hear your cries.
I wipe your tears. I calm you in times of anger.

I give you hope when you need courage. I give you joy in times of sorrow.

Your happiness is My happiness. Your love is My love.
Your heart is My heart. Your peace is My peace.

I give you abundance in times of need.
I give you eyes to see, ears to hear, hands to touch.
I give you a smile to turn to laughter.

When you do not know the way, I Am your compass.
When enemies attack, I Am your shield.

In times of darkness, I Am your light.

■■■

I do not expect anything you are not capable of.
I know you can feel. I know you can love because I created this in you.

I gave you mouths to speak My word.
I gave you lips to kiss, to provide an opening from your heart to My heart.

I will lift you so you may lift others.
I will comfort you so you may comfort others.
I will love you so you may love others.
I will give you peace so you may calm others.
I will give you food so you may feed others.

When they are hungry, I am hungry. I will fill your cup. I will provide.

I do not expect you to understand My work.
I understand you. I created you.

I know you can love, I gave you love. I Am love.
I know you are beautiful, I gave you beauty. I Am beauty.
I know you are strong, I gave you strength. I Am strength.

Your happiness is My happiness.
Your peace is My peace.
Your joy is My joy.
Your love is My love.
Your wisdom is My wisdom.
Your courage is My courage.

I feel what you feel. I Am always with you.

Your mind is a portal to My mind.
Your soul is a window to My soul.
Your heart beats as My heart.

I hear you. I know you are afraid. Do not be afraid.

Your strength comes from Me.
Your courage comes from Me.
Your wisdom comes from Me.

■■■

The world listens when I speak.

I will give you the words to say when you do not know what to say.
I will give you the courage to believe when you do not believe.

I will open your heart when you do not feel.

I will provide a way where there is no way.
I will provide a map when you are lost.

I will give you food when you are hungry.

I will show you love.
I will show you joy.
I will show you abundance.

I will provide you comfort.
I will provide you strength.
I will provide you courage.

I will provide light when there is darkness.
I will provide silence when there is noise.
I will provide the boat to travel My ocean.
I will provide your feet the strength to walk My path.

I will help your eyes to see to help others to see.

I will give you taste so others can taste.
I will give you music so you may dance.

■■■

My power knows no limits.

I Am space. I Am time. I Am love. I Am eternity.
I Am the sun. I Am the stars. I Am the moon.

I Am in you. You are in Me. We are all One.

Your breath is My breath. Your heart is My heart.
Your love is My love. Your joy is My joy.

I Am your rock. I Am your strength.
You are My pride. You are My joy.

I hear your cries when others do not.

When enemies surround you, I Am your protection.

I keep you safe so you may slumber. I Am your heat when you are cold.

I Am your heart. You are My heart. We are One.

YOU ARE MY GREATEST CREATION

Be thankful for Me. I Am thankful for you.
Be loving to Me. I always love you.
Be caring to others, because your care is My care.

I Am light. I Am in you. I Am everywhere.

I Am all knowing when you do not know.

Your breath is My breath. Your feet are My feet.

I Am what is on your path and what is in your heart.

I fill you from the overflow.

Your riches are My riches. You dance to My music.

■■■

All of My power is already in you and in everyone, in all living creatures, now and then, and in the future.

I Am here for you. You are here for Me.
You will always be mine. I will always be yours.

I Am light. I Am love. I Am strength. I Am beauty.

I Am the stars in the sky. I Am everywhere and in everyone.

You give Me joy. You give Me laughter.

Your pain is My pain. Your tears are My tears.

Your wisdom comes from Me. I give you the strength to persevere.

When you say, "Thank you, I have enough," I will provide more than you can ever imagine.

Your time is My time. Know that you are always in the right time and space because I Am time and space.

▪▪▪

My message is abundance.
My message is hope.
My message is love.

Spread My message so there is more abundance.
Share My hope so there is more hope.
Speak My greatness so I may show My wonder.

▪▪▪

You are My love. I will always love you even when you do not love Me.

I will give you courage when you fear.
I will calm your doubts when you worry.
I will show up when you call My name.

When your enemies do not believe, I will make them believe because I made them in My image just as I made you.

Your possibility is My possibility.
Your gratitude is My gratitude.
My blessing is your prayer.

I know the answer before you ask the question.

Just know. I Am always here. I will never leave you.

You will never leave Me even when you cannot see Me.
You will hear Me even if you choose not to listen.

Your breath is My breath.
Your heart is My heart.
Your love is My love.

I Am eternity and you are My beloved.

I Am in the animals on land. I Am in the fish in the sea.

I Am in the stars in the sky. I Am the sun that shines.

My love warms your Earth. My power calms your fears.

I Am always near because I Am everywhere and because I love you.

■■■

You are My greatest creation because I gave you the capacity to love Me.

I gave you the courage to walk in My path.

I gave you eyes so you may see Me.
I gave you ears so you may hear Me.

I gave you a voice so you can call My name and speak My word.

I gave you the power to believe so I may show you miracles.

I gave you money so you may experience riches, and love so you can experience My wisdom.

I gave you a heart that beats so you may feel Me.
I gave you lungs to breathe so you know I Am the air.

I gave you stars in the sky so you may have the courage to dream.

I gave you sleep so you may wake.

I gave you feet so you may rise up and proclaim My name to all who listen.

I gave you a mind so you may have the ability to change, to always seek My knowledge. To know more. To know Me.

I Am in you. I Am everywhere. I Am in everyone.

I Am eternity. I Am love. I Am joy.

Your grief is My grief. Your pain is My pain.

Know that I Am always here for you, here with you, even when you do not see Me, even when you are afraid to believe. I have faith in you even when you do not have faith in Me, because you are mine. You are My beloved.

I know the answer before you ask the question because I Am The Answer.

You are My child. Your children are My children.

I will always keep you safe.
I will always provide shelter in times of storms.
I will always provide sustenance in times of famine.
I Am always with you since you are in Me and we are all One.

There is no need to tremble and be afraid because I love you now and always, in all space and time because I Am space and time.

My power knows no bounds.
My love has no walls.
My heart has no fear.
My mind has no worry.

I Am your strength and you are mine.

BE BOLD AND I WILL DANCE WITH YOU

Freedom is for everyone. I created everyone in My image.

I want happiness for all. I want peace for all.

Love is everywhere.
Love is in all things and all people and all time.
Love is My creation and My desire for you.

▪▪▪

Relax and be still.

Trust in Me. I trust in you. I created you.

Follow Me. I will lead.
Listen to Me. I will be your guide.
Love with Me. I will offer you My protection.
Walk with Me, so I may carry you.
Speak with Me, so I may listen. I hear you.

I hear you when you call My name. I Am here.
I feel when you are frightened. I Am love.
I smile when I wipe your tears. I Am joy.

I will guide you when you are lost. I Am strength.
I will show you a way when there is no way.
I will create a path for you to walk when there is no path.
I will carry you when you stumble and are weary.

I Am energy. I Am light. I conquer darkness.

I Am happy. I Am joy.
I Am beauty. I Am wonder. I Am awe.
I Am in all things and all people and all time.

I Am in you. You are in Me. We are all One.

■■■

Listen when I call you.

Do not be afraid of My commands.

I will direct your steps.

I will give you the words to say, the mouth to speak, your feet to move so you may carry My word, My message.

My message is love. My message is opportunity.

My message is hope in times of despair.
My message is strength in times of weakness.
My message is love in times of hate.
My message is joy in times of sadness.
My message is beauty in times of darkness.

When your heart speaks, people will listen.

Your heart is My heart.
Your breath is My breath.
Your feet are My feet.

I will carry you when you do not know the way. I Am The Way.

I Am the stars in the sky. I Am the birds in the trees. I Am the fish in the ocean. I Am the sun that warms you and the wind that cools you.

I love you always.
You are mine and I Am yours.
I Am in you and you are in Me. We are One.

Together we are unstoppable.

▪▪▪

Do My work. I will reward you with riches and abundance beyond belief.

Believe and you will see.
Dream and you will wake.
Rise up and you will walk.
Love and you will be loved.

I will always love you. I Am love.
I will always guide you. I Am strength.
I will always adore you. You are mine.

We are One. We are together always.
No one or no thing can destroy us or divide us.

Together we are unstoppable.

▪▪▪

Earth follows My path. I Am the path.
Boats navigate My oceans. I Am the water.

I Am shelter from storms.

I Am the leaves on the trees. I Am the grass on the ground.
I Am the sand on the shore. I Am the waves on the oceans.
I Am the sun in the sky. I Am the moon and the stars.

I Am in you. You are in Me. We are One.

Together we are unstoppable.

▪▪▪

Follow My commands and I will guide you.
Love all people and you will know no enemies.
Speak greatness and you will be greatness.
Walk My path and you will never be lost.

Listen to Me and you will know what to say.
Listen to others and you will know what to hear.

When babies cry, I Am their comfort.
When you are old, I will comfort your fears.

Do not be frightened. I Am always with you.
You are never alone even when you feel alone.

I feel you even when you do not feel Me.
I hear you even when you do not hear Me.

I will speak for you when you do not know the words to say.

People will listen. They will hear My message.

My message is love. I Am love.
My message is beauty. I Am beauty.
My message is wonder. I Am wonder.
My message is abundance. I Am abundance.
My message is clear. I Am clarity.

Speak and I will listen.
Listen and I will speak.
Cry and I will comfort you.
Laugh and I will be happy with you.
Be glad and I will be thankful for you.

You are mine. I Am yours. We are One.

■■■

Be merry and I will sing with you.
Be bold and I will dance with you.
Be joyful and I will laugh with you.
Be grateful and I will reward you.

Listen and I will show you the way.

Where there is no way, I will make a way.
Where there is no path, I will make a path.
Where there is no bridge, I will build a bridge.

You shall never cross troubled waters when you follow My way.
I Am the water.

You will never grow tired when you are doing My work.

I Am the light and the sun that gives you energy and power.

When clouds appear, I Am still near.

I Am the clouds and the rain and the moon and the stars.

I Am all the planets and all the galaxies.
I Am all space and all time.

I Am all knowing and all seeing.

I Am God. You are mine. Together we are One.

I AM THE JOY YOU EXPERIENCE

You are My beloved. I created you so you may do My work and carry out My mission and speak My message.

Know that I Am here.
Know that I Am always near.

Know that I always listen.
Know that I always give you the words to say.

Know that I will always wipe your tears.
Know that I will always carry you to keep your feet from stumbling.
Know that I will always protect you from storms.
Know that I will always guide you and love you.

I created you. I created space. I created time.

My work is your work.
My work will not be complete unless you do My work.

My love will not be complete unless you share My love.

My heart will not expand unless you breathe My air.
My music will not be heard unless you sing My song.
My wonders will not be seen unless you speak of My magic.
My miracles will not appear unless you describe My wonders.

I Am the light. I Am the wonders.
I Am the beauty. I Am the awe.

I Am the day. I Am the night.
I Am the stars. I Am the sky.

I Am in you. You are in Me. Together we are One.

■■■

Be not afraid. I shall protect you.

Do not worry. I will lift you from confusion.
Do not be anxious. I will open your mind and heart.
Do not be scared. I will free your burdens.
Do not be angry. I will give you love.

Do not fear. I will show you the way. I Am The Way.

Do not be afraid to live. I Am life.
Do not be afraid to dream. I Am your dreams.
Do not be afraid to love. I Am love.
Do not be afraid to soar. I Am the sky.
Do not be afraid to travel. I Am the stars to light your path.
Do not be afraid to give. I Am power.
Do not be afraid to receive. I Am abundance.
Do not be afraid to create. I Am beauty.

You are mine. I Am yours. Together we are One.

■■■

I Am the moon. I Am the sun.
I Am the land. I Am the ocean.

I Am the air you breathe and the words you say.
I Am the blood in your veins and the beating of your heart.

I gave you eyes to see and lips to speak.
I gave you feet to walk and music to dance.

I gave you dreams to discover, and power to wonder, and gifts to give so you may receive My love.

I Am love. I Am beauty. I Am joy. I Am wonder. I Am awe.

I Am in you. You are in Me. Together we are One.

■■■

I Am the joy you experience.

I Am the laughter when you smile.
I Am the comfort when you cry.
I Am the shelter from your storms.

I Am the thunder when you need to hear.
I Am the power when you need to move.
I Am the rhythm when you need to dance.
I Am the music when you need to celebrate.
I Am the art when you need to create.
I Am the beauty when you need to love.

I Am your strength when you are weary.

I Am your air when it is time to soar.

I Am the stars when you need to believe.

I Am peace when you are anxious.
I Am calm when you are afraid.
I Am knowledge when you need wisdom.
I Am here when you call out My name.

I Am The Answer before you ask the question.

I Am always here for you.

I Am in you. You are in Me. Together we are One.

■■■

I Am living. I Am alive. I Am free.
I Am healthy. I Am able. I Am willing.
I Am happiness. I Am beauty.

I Am The Creator of all things, all people, all planets, all galaxies, all stars, all suns, all moons, all that ever will be and all that ever was.

I Am the breath you breathe and your heart that beats.
I Am your feet that move you and your eyes so you may see the way.

I Am your ears so you may hear Me.
I Am your mouth so you may speak My word.

Share My magic. Share My wonders so I may share with you and all peoples and all of My creations.

Speak of My beauty. Speak of My love.

I will guide you. I Am your rock.
I Am your protection from fear and deliverance from evil.

I Am happiness so you may experience happiness.
I Am joy so you may experience joy.
I Am wonder so you may know wonder.
I Am love so you may feel My love.
I Am beauty so you may create My art.
I Am miracles so you may know of My possibilities.

My power is endless. My magic is unstoppable.

I can move mountains. I can shine sun and stars.
I will make a way when there is no way.

I Am in all things, all people, all space and all time. I Am space. I Am time.

I Am peace. I Am love. I Am power. I Am abundance. I Am beauty.

You are mine and I Am yours and together we are One.

I AM ALL POSSIBILITY

Love so I may love you.
Forgive so I may redeem you.
Value so I may reward you.
Give so I may share with you.

Create so I may demonstrate My magic.
Dream so I may deliver My miracles.

Taste so I may feed you.
Drink so I may sustain you.

Walk so I may carry you.

Do not worry. I will calm you.
Do not fear. I will protect you.
Do not harm. I will guide you.

Move and I will move with you.
Dream and I will dream with you.

My love and My power know no boundaries.
My skies and My galaxies know no limits.

My possibilities are endless.

I Am All There Is, all there ever was and all there will ever be.
I Am in you. You are in Me. Together we are One.

▪▪▪

All things are possible when you believe.
All dreams come true when you wake.
All love is real when you share My love.
All truth is real when you speak My words.
All hearts are real when all peoples join as one.

▪▪▪

I know you can do great things because I Am greatness and My greatness is in you.

I Am your power. I Am your confidence.
I Am your love. I Am your beauty.

I made you in My image.

Go out and be born.
Jump and be lifted.
Cry out and be free.
Stumble and I will carry you.

You are in Me. I Am in you. Together we are One.

▪▪▪

All possibilities are My possibilities. I Am possibility.
All journeys travel My roads. I Am The Way.

I Am your light. I Am your guide.
I Am your shelter. I Am your protector.

I Am your redeemer when you lose your way.
I Am your rock when you need strength.
I Am your bread when you need sustenance.
I Am your love when you give My love.
I Am your power when you share My power.
I Am your wonder when you wake from your dreams.
I Am your beauty when you create My art.
I Am your music when you dance.
I Am your sun when you need light.
I Am your air when you breathe.

You will never drown in My oceans. I will protect you.
You will never be lost on your journeys. I Am your way.
You will never be afraid or confused. I Am peace. I Am clarity.

I Am everywhere. I Am in everything.
I Am in every creature now, or ever was, or will be.
I Am in all space and time because I Am space and time.

You are in Me. I Am in you. Together we are One.

■■■

"Show me the way," you ask, and I will show you.
"Give me love," and I will love you.
"Provide me power," and I will power you.

I will move you when you are tired.
I will comfort you when you are afraid.
I will dry your tears in times of sadness.
I will light your way in times of darkness.
I will protect you from evil.

I Am peace. I Am love. I Am beauty.
I Am joy. I Am abundance.
I Am the sun. I Am the stars. I Am the sky.
I Am the moon. I Am the planets. I Am the galaxies.
I Am all space and all time.

I created everything and everyone.

Nothing is impossible because I Am all possibility.

I Am beauty. You are beautiful to Me.
I Am love. You are lovely to Me.

I Am grateful when you are thankful for Me.

I give you riches when you share My wealth.
I give you words when you speak My knowledge.

I Am your truth when you seek My answers.

I Am your strength in times of weakness.
I Am your laughter in times of joy.

I Am your freedom in times of injustice.
I Am your rights in times of wrongs.
I Am your redeemer in times of troubles.
I Am your health in times of sickness.
I Am your peace in times of war.
I Am your thanksgiving in times of jealousy.
I Am your calm in times of rage.

I Am your power. I Am your gladness.

I power you. I Am glad for you.

You are mine. I Am yours. Together we are One.

YOU ARE MY BELOVED

Love is My creation.
Beauty is My creation.

You are My creation.

I created you so you may share My beauty and share My love.
I sustain you so you may walk in My path and speak of My miracles.

I will show you the way when there is no way.
I will make a beginning when there is an ending.
I will make music when you need to dance.
I will make a song when you need to sing.
I will give you joy when you need to laugh.

I will shower you with gifts so you may be thankful.
I will provide you riches so you may know abundance.
I will be the water so you may travel My oceans.
I will be the air so you may soar in My skies.
I will inspire you to dream and to create.

I know no limits.

I Am all wonder. I Am all beauty.
I Am all time. I Am all space.

You are mine. I Am yours.
Together we are One.

▪▪▪

Be happy for I Am happy.
Be loving for I Am love.
Be generous for I Am generosity.
Be comforting for I Am comfort.
Be joyful for I Am joy.
Be glad for I Am gladness.
Be beauty for I Am beauty.
Be abundance for I Am abundance.
Be giving for I Am sharing.
Be believing for I believe in you.

I created you.

Stay in truth for I Am true.
Walk in My path for I Am The Way.
Love your neighbor for I Am in everyone.

Be fruitful for I Am creation.
Be happy for I know no sadness.
Be hopeful for I know no limits.

Dream the impossible and I will make it possible.

My power has no ends. I have no boundaries.

I Am all space and time.
I Am in you. You are in Me.
Together we are One.

▪▪▪

I give so you may share My generosity.
I love so you may share My love.
I speak so you shall know My truth.
I comfort so you shall know My protection.
I create so you may create.
I sing so you may dance.
I make a way so you will never be lost.
I provide the answer so you will never be confused.

I Am clarity when you are anxious.
I Am freedom when you are troubled.

I Am the words you speak.
I Am the air you breathe.
I Am the stars that shine in your skies.
I Am the dream inside you.
I Am the possibility that awakens you.
I Am the magic that electrifies you.

I Am your energy. I Am your power.

I drive you. I move you.

When you move, I Am moved.

When you believe, I Am here for you.

I Am always here for you even when you do not believe.

I Am everywhere. I Am in everyone. I Am in every living creature.

You are made in My image.

You are My greatest creation because I gave you the power to believe, the courage to dream, the generosity to give, the music to dance.

You are My beloved.

WONDER IS EVERYWHERE

I am clear. I am confident. I am led.
I am strong. I am able. I am willing.
I am whole. I am complete.
I have energy. I have drive.
I have enthusiasm. I have creativity.
I am loving. I am beautiful.
I am capable. I am joyful. I am thankful.

I trust. I move. I soar.
I fly. I sing. I dance.
I share. I give. I receive.

I am abundant. I am energized.
I am magnetized with spirit.

God is in me and I am in God.

I am thankful. I have all that I need.

▪▪▪

Where there is no way, God will make a way.
Where there are no words, God will give me the words to speak.

When there is no love, God will give me love to share what is in my heart with others so they may feel what I feel and know what I know and be joyful as I am joyful and be full of thanksgiving and wonder and awe.

▪▪▪

Miracles happen when we believe. I believe.
Dreams come true when we wake. I am awake.
Knowledge rings true when we are aware. I am aware.
Courage transforms us when we are ready. I am ready.
God triumphs when He leads us. Lead me.
God reigns when we trust in Him. I trust.
Confidence moves us when we are inspired. I am confident.

▪▪▪

Possibilities are endless. God is endless.
Wonder is everywhere. God is everywhere.

I am happy. God is happy.
I am loving. God is love.
I am beautiful. God is beauty.
I am wise. God is knowledge.
I am powerful. God is power.

God is my rock and my shield.
God is my protector and my provider.
God is my shelter and my home.

I am clear. I am confident. I am led.

God loves me no matter what I do. He is with me always.

I am clear, I am confident, I am led.

I may stumble when I do not know the way but God will always show me the way. I may be deaf and will not hear, yet God will always listen.

My voice may be weak but God will always give me the words to say. My feet may stumble on the path, yet God will build a bridge for me to cross.

I shall explore His lands.
I shall travel His oceans.
I shall wonder at His stars.
I shall warm myself in the light of His sun.

I shall dream at night and wake in the morning, thankful for all I have, all He has given me.

▪▪▪

Love knows no bounds. Freedom knows no limits.

God's skies are endless. God's time is eternal.
God's magic is full of wonder and awe.
God Is All There Is and all there will ever be.

I am one with God.

I am one with the universe and all of His creations.
I am one with the moon and the stars.

I am one with all time and space because God is all time and space
and I am one with God.

There is nothing that God cannot do.

God is unstoppable. God can move mountains and uproot trees.
God can show us love and peace in times of hatred and war.

God loves us no matter what. God knows us more than we can imagine.

God's possibilities are endless.
God's wonders know no bounds.
God's truth is ageless.
God's wisdom is perfect.
God's magic astounds us.
God's heat warms us.

God never ceases to create.

We are His creations. We are here to do His work.

▪▪▪

God never leaves us. God supports us.

We succeed because of God's love.
We enlighten our world because of God's wisdom.
We love one another with the warmth of God's love.
We are complete because we are made whole with God.

■■■

Behold, all things are new because God never runs out of space. He is space. Behold, all things are possible because God never runs out of time. He is time.

God Is All There Is and all there will ever be.

I am one with God. We are all One.

■■■

God is my biggest fan.

He is my rock. He is my savior from troubled waters.

Storms rise yet God never leaves us.
Earth may tremble yet God protects us.
Our cries may grow silent yet God always hears us.

His love is perfect. His works are pure.
His creations are complete. His magic is ceaseless.
His wonders always amaze. His love always embraces us.
His words always calm us. His power always shields us from harm.

We are enveloped in His love.
We are made whole through His goodness.
We hear him when we call His name.

He hears us when we listen, now and always.

His possibilities are endless. We are endless.
His magic is miraculous. We are miraculous.
His stars shine in the sky. We shine on His earth.

His sun lights our path. Our feet carry us across His lands.

His waters sustain us. We travel across His oceans.

God keeps us safe. He is our safety.
God protects us from evil. He is our refuge.
God loves us. God hears us.

Now and always, God is All There Is.

WE ARE BOUNDLESS

Truth knows no limits because God knows no limits.
Love never expires because God never expires.
Creation never ceases because God never ceases.

God Is All There Is and all there will ever be.

God hears us in times of troubles and calms us when we cry.

God comforts us when we are afraid, and shows us a way where there is no way. God always makes a way.

God lights our path in times of darkness.
God lifts us up in times of trouble.

God is always here for us. We are always here for God.

We are One with God.

■■■

God Is All There Is.

God reigns through all space and time because God is space and time.

God created us to do His work and proclaim His miracles.
God uses us to show His magic and share His love.
God asks us to harness His power to accomplish great things.

God loves us in times of hate.
God strengthens us in times of weakness.
God lights us in times of darkness.
God calms us in times of fear.
God protects us in times of trouble.

Waters may rise yet God never leaves us.
Oceans may roar yet God never lets us drown.
Storms rage yet God shields us from destruction.

Space is endless. God is endless.
Time is limitless. God is limitless.
We are boundless. God is boundless.

God Is All There Is and all there will ever be, now and always.

We are One with God.

▪▪▪

Enemies will quake when they meet God's magic.

The earth will tremble yet God is always near.

He is here when we do not hear Him.
He sees us when we do not see Him.

He protects us. He lifts us. He loves us.

God made us. God needs us. We need God. We are One.

God Is All There Is, now and always.

We are One with God.

▪▪▪

God's love is eternal. We are eternal.
God's heart beats forever. We live forever.
God's thoughts move the earth. We move with God.

He leads us. He carries us. He surrounds us.
He is in us and we are in Him.

God needs us. God loves us.

God will always show us the way.

Where there is no way, He will make a way.

Where there are oceans, God will build us a boat.
Where there are valleys to cross, God will build us a bridge.

When there is no food to eat, God will provide sustenance.

When we need strength, God gives us strength. He is our strength.
When we need love, God gives us love. He is our love.
When we need wisdom, God shares His truth. He is our truth.
When we need air to breathe, God fills our lungs. He is our breath.
When we need words to speak, God gives us His voice. We are His voice.

God's energy is endless. His works are timeless.

His miracles fill us with wonder and awe.

He fills our cup when we are thirsty.
He fills our plates when we are hungry.

He opens doors when we are stuck.
He builds bridges when we are scared.

He rescues us in times of trouble. He is our redeemer and our salvation.

God loves us no matter what.

God Is All There Is.
We are One with God.

■■■

We always win when we enter God's race.

God's course is pure. His heart full of magic.

He shares His magic so we may proclaim His power.
His energy powers us. He moves us.
His works always amaze. He inspires us. He lifts us.

When we are weak, He is our strength.
When we are troubled, He is our calm.
When we are confused, He is our clarity.
When we are lost, He is our salvation.

He is happy when we share His love.
He is joyful when we proclaim His miracles.
He is peaceful when we glorify His wonders.

He hears us when we call His name.
He sees us when we look up at His stars.
He carries us across His oceans.

He marvels with us when we share His greatness.
He stands with us when we need strength to move.
He rises with us when we need power to overcome obstacles.
He cries with us when we are lonely and afraid.
He is here with us always. He never leaves us.

▪▪▪

I know God is with me always.

I know God loves me always.
I know God protects me always.
I know God saves me always.

I know God is joyful always.

I know God shares His wisdom always. He is truth.
I know God shares His riches always. He is abundance.
I know God moves us always. He is our energy.
I know God's heart is limitless because His love is endless.

I know God drives us. I know God hears us.

I know God knows us.

God created us.

We are One with God.

DO NOT BE AFRAID

Do not be afraid. I will always protect you.
Do not be hateful. I will always love you.
Do not be silent. I will always hear you.
Do not grow weary. I will always power you.

Do not be lost for I Am always found.

I Am everywhere. I Am All There Is and all there will ever be.

I created you so you may proclaim My miracles. I carry you so you may spread My word, and all people will marvel at My wonders. I perform miracles so you will believe.

When you believe, all things are possible, for I Am possibility.
When you love, I Am here, for I Am love.
When you are thankful, I Am here, for I Am amazement.
When you have sinned, I Am here, for I Am forgiveness.
When you hurt another, I Am here, for I Am protection.
When you walk My path, I Am here, for I Am power.
When you are sick, I Am here, for I Am health.

I Am time. I Am space. I Am earth.
I Am the stars. I Am the sky. I Am the ocean.
I Am the birds. I Am the trees.
I Am the fish. I Am the seas.

I Am in people. I Am in you.
You are in Me. Together we are One.

GRATITUDE IS FUEL, LOVE IS FIRE

We are unstoppable because God is unstoppable.
We are powerful because God is powerful.
We are loving because God is kind.
We are made new because God forgives.
We are washed clean because God is the water.

We breathe in possibility because God is the air.

We soar because God lifts us. We walk because God carries us.

We are thankful because God provides for us.
We are content because God sustains us.

God performs His magic when we believe.
God lights our way in times of darkness.

We have the answers because God is truth.

God has the answers before we ask the questions, because God Is All There Is and all there ever will be.

■■■

We float on the wave of God.
We fly in the sky of God.
We swim in the ocean of God.
We walk on the lands of God.
We love with the peoples of God.

God loves all people, for He created all people.

We are all made in His image. We are here to do great things.

God is here to perform great miracles.

▪▪▪

God loves us. God watches over us.

God always hears us when we cry out for Him, and when we do not.

God moves us when we are weak and when we are strong. God carries us when we are tired and when we have strength. God is our strength.

God is our salvation when we need to forgive because God forgives.

God never abandons us when we are lost.

God always feeds us when we are hungry.

God fills our cup when we are thirsty. His water is living water.

▪▪▪

Our mind is God's mind. He is our knowledge.
Our heart is God's heart. He is our love.
Our ears are God's ears. He hears us. He listens.
Our hope is God's hope. He is our possibility.
Our feet are God's feet. He stands with us.
Our energy is God's energy. He moves us.

God is thankful for us, for we are thankful for God.

We glorify His name and marvel at His stars.
We are warmed by His sun, for God is light.

God is our escape from times of trouble.

God is our path where there is no path.

Where there is no path, God will make a path.

Where there is no love, God will share His love.
Where there is no truth, God will share His wisdom.
Where there is no peace, God will expand our hearts.

When we do not see, God will provide our vision.
When we do not hear, God will listen.

▪▪▪

God knows the answer before we ask the question, for God is the answer to questions never asked.

God is the solution for problems never solved.

God is perfect. God is pure.
God is holy. We are holy.
God is loving. We are loving.
God is awesome. We are filled with awe.
God is wonder. We are amazed.
God is power. We are powerful.

God is our rock. He is our strength.

He Is All There Is. He is always with us.

We are always in God. We are One.

▪▪▪

Stand back for God is coming. Be near for God is already here.

God provides for us. God loves us.

God needs us to do great things, for God is greatness and we are One with God.

God is possibility. We are possibility.

All things are possible in the mind of God.
All things are seen in the eyes of God.
All things are heard in the ears of God.
All things are moved by the power of God.
All things are energized by the light of God.
All things are lifted out of darkness by God's might.

Clouds may appear. God never disappears.
Waters may rise. God never drowns.

God always reigns. He is supreme.

He is justice. He is kindness.
He is love in times of hate.
He is calm in times of fear.
He is food in times of hunger.
He is water in times of drought.
He is art in times of magic.
He is beauty in times of ugliness.
He is grateful in times of thanksgiving.

Gratitude is fuel. Love is fire.

God is magical. He is miraculous.
God is amazement. He is wonder.
God is energy. He is power.
God is clear. He is truth.
God is strength. He is unstoppable.
God is constant. He is unshakeable.
God is eternal. He is endless.
God is space. God is time.

God Is All There Is.

We are One.

■■■

We sit on God's shore and marvel at His oceans.
We walk on God's path and are moved by His power.
We share God's love and are amazed by His works.
We proclaim God's truth and are comforted by His answer.

God is the answer before we ask the question. God knows all.

God needs us. God hears us.

God cries for us when we are sad.
God celebrates with us when we are happy.
God clears our minds when we are filled with confusion.

God is our rock when we need strength.

He is our shield in times of trouble, and our health when we are sick.

God champions us when we need to believe.

He shines His stars when we need to see.
He opens our mouths when we need to speak.

He gives us the words to say when we do not have the words.
He gives us the love to share when we have no love.
He gives us hearts to feel when our minds are closed.

When we feel trapped, He is our escape.

When we are tired, God wakes us.
When we stumble, God carries us.
When we need protection, God saves us.

God Is All There Is and all there will ever be.

THERE ARE ONLY BEGINNINGS

Speak and I shall listen.
Hope and I will provide.
Believe and I will amaze.

I Am God.

You are in Me and I Am in you.

Together we are One. Together we are unstoppable.

I Am All There Is.

You are My creation.

I need you to carry out My work and to spread My word.

My message is love. My message is opportunity.
My message is wonder. My message is awe.

Carry forth My message and I will provide for you.

Proclaim My greatness. Share My magic. Show My love.

Rise up from your slumber so your dreams may come true.

Open your ears so you may hear Me.
Open your eyes so you may see Me.
Open your heart and let Me in so I may do great things.

Listen when I call as I always hear you.
Love all your neighbors as I created all of you.

I Am The Answer before you ask the question.
I Am God. You are in Me and I Am in you.

Together we are One.

■■■

Division is not possible for I Am everywhere.
Strife is not possible for I Am peace.
Worry is not possible for I Am calm.
Lack is not possible for I Am abundance.
Limitation is not possible for I Am endless.
Endings are not possible for I Am all time.

There are only beginnings. There are endless tomorrows.
There are inventions to create. There is love to attract.
There is hope to spread and power to believe.

I will always take care of you. I will provide for you.

You have nothing to fear for I Am always with you.
You have nothing to be shameful for as I always forgive.

When you cry out, I hear you. I always hear you.
When you share, I love you. I always love you.
When you believe, My magic appears. I Am magic.
When you grow tired, I power you. I Am power.
When you are trapped, I free you. I Am freedom.

Listen when I call and I will provide.

Spread My message and I will light your way.
Proclaim My miracles and I will show you greatness.

Be thankful. Be grateful. I Am grateful for I created you.

You are made in My likeness and image.
You came to this earth to accomplish greatness.
You love on this earth to share My love and show others the way.

▪▪▪

Speak and I will listen.
Believe and I will provide.
Wonder and I will amaze.
Imagine and I will create.

Hope and I shall do the impossible.
Speak and I shall provide the words to say.
Walk and I shall provide the strength to move.

My love is eternal. You are eternal.
My message is freedom. You are free.

Together we are great.

We are unstoppable. We know no limits. We are designed to soar.

All I Am, you are. You are in Me and I Am in you.

Together we are One.

Love one another. Be kind to one another, for I Am love and kindness.

Share My word and speak My truth, for I Am The Answer.

My message is pure. My message is eternal.

I Am time. I Am space.

I Am All There Is.

I Am God.

GOD IS READY, GOD IS AVAILABLE

Where there is love, there is God. Where there is hope, there is God.

Where there are miracles, there is God, for only God can perform miracles.

Where there is opportunity, there is God, for God is limitless possibility.

Where there is energy, there is God, for God is indescribable power.

God is inaudible. He is in the seen and unseen.
God is inexhaustible. He is eternal. He is endless.

God Is All There Is.

Together we are One.

■■■

Lift my eyes, so I may see.
Hear my cries, so I may persevere.
Move my feet, so I can carry out Your work.
Deliver me from evil so I may spread Your love.
Provide me answers so I am never lost.

Deliver Your miracles and I am filled with wonder.

I am filled with hope.
I am filled with possibility.
I am filled with laughter.

All sadness is gone.
All worry is gone.
All hate is gone.
All fear is gone.

God Is All There Is and all there will ever be.

For this I am thankful.

▪▪▪

I trust in God.

I stand with God, for God stands with me.

I am filled with love. God is love.
I speak words of wisdom. God is truth.
I triumph over evil. God is mighty.
I share my greatness. God is great.
I look up at the heavens. God is wonderful.

Wherever I am, God is.

Whenever I love, God loves.
Whenever I trust, God reigns supreme.

God Is All There Is. I am one with God.

God is one with me. Together we are One.

God is freedom. I am free.
God is opportunity. I am thankful.

▪▪▪

All things are possible in the mind of God.

I am possibility. I am His creation.

I am perfect. I am whole. I am complete.

God is perfect. God is whole. God is complete.

I am love. I am joy. I am beauty.

God is love. God is joy. God is beauty.

I am wonderful. I am amazing.

God is wonder. God is awe.

God provides and sustains.

God is hope. God is courage.

I am hopeful. I am courageous.

I am unstoppable when I move with God.

God moves with me. God is in me.

God is in us. God is in everything.

Together we are One.

▪▪▪

Miracles arrive when you are open to them.

I am ready. I am available.
We are ready. We are available.
God is ready. God is available.

EVERYTHING IS ALIVE

I Am God. I Am available.

I Am always here for you. I Am always with you.

I stand with you. I carry you. I light your way. I light your life.

I Am The Light. I Am Life.

I created all life in My image and likeness.

Humanity is My greatest creation.

You can love Me. You can hear Me. You can feel Me.

I know this because I created this in you.

Just be open and allow Me to touch you.

I know you feel. I know your heart will be moved.

I hear it beating. I hear you breathing.

I Am here with you always.

I Am in you. You are in Me.

Together we are One.

■■■

All there is, is Life itself. Life is all there is.

Everything is alive:

The stars in the sky
The fish in the sea
The clouds in the heavens
The thunder that roars
The waves that crash

The love that protects you
The care that warms your soul
The joy that eases your pain
The miracles that end your suffering

I do not want you to suffer. I Am not suffering.
I do not want you to hurt. I Am not hurting.
I do not want you to know pain. I Am not pain.

I Am joy. I Am beauty. I Am gladness.
I Am tranquility. I Am peace. I Am love.

I Am All There Is. Life is All There Is.

We are. Together we are One.

■■■

I Am in you. I created you.

Love is in you. I created love.
Joy is in you. I created joy.

Health is in you. I Am health.
Peace is in you. I Am peace.
Creation is in you. I Am creation.

I created you. I created all.

I create all love.
I protect all sadness.
I heal all sickness.

I always hear your prayers.

When you call My name, I protect you.
When you believe in My powers, I astound you.
When you trust in Me, I trust you.

I trust you because I created you.

I Am Creation.

I Am all space and time.

I Am the earth and the moon.
I Am the sun and the clouds.
I Am the stars and the galaxies.
I Am the fish and the oceans.

I Am waters. I Am lands.

I Am in all life.

Life is all there is. I Am All There Is.

You are in Me. I Am in you.

Together we are One.

■■■

Life moves in waves. Energy moves in waves.

I Am life. I Am energy.

I Am light when you feel darkness.
I Am clarity when you feel confusion.
I Am joy when you feel sadness.
I Am love when you feel openness.
I Am peace when you feel struggle.
I Am heat when you feel coldness.

I Am here for you.

I always will protect you.

Believe in Me. I believe in you.

Love Me. I love you.

Hear Me. I hear you.

See Me everywhere, in everyone and everything. I see you.

I Am everywhere. I Am in everyone.

I created all. I created you.

You are in Me. I Am in you.

I Am All There Is.

Together we are One.

THERE ARE NO MISTAKES

Do not be upset. There are no mistakes.
Do not be closed. There is only openness.
Do not be hateful. There is only love.
Do not be sad. There is only happiness.
Do not be poor. There is only abundance.
Do not be hurtful. There is only peace.
Do not be lost. There is only The Way.

I Am The Way. I Am life. I Am light.

I Am the sun. I Am the stars.
I Am the earth. I Am the moon.
I Am the waters. My love is living water.

I Am peace. My heart beats for you.
I Am time. My guidance shows you the way for I Am The Way.

I Am All There Is.

For this, there is only one way as all paths lead to Me.

When you are lost, I will show you the correct path.

When you are afraid, I will give you courage.
When you cannot stand, I will give you the power to walk.

When you feel pain, I comfort you.
When you feel joy, I celebrate with you.

When you create, I create.
When you love, I love.
When you feel, I feel.
When you feel Me, I show up.

I Am in you always whether you believe in Me or not. I believe in you.

I protect you always whether you are in danger or not. I Am courage.
I celebrate with you, whether you feel joy or not. I Am joy.

I guide you whether you are lost or not. I Am guidance. I Am The Way.

▪▪▪

I do not destroy, only create.
I do not hurt, only heal.
I do not close, only open.
I do not confuse, only guide.
I do not hate, only love.
I do not withhold, only provide.

I forgive. I believe in you.

I Am light in darkness.
I Am protection in troubles.

I never repeat.

I Am only original.

You are original.

I Am in you.
You are in Me.

I Am All There Is.

We are original.

▪▪▪

I only allow. I do not scorn.

You are My channel. You are My vessel.
Your cup is filled with My water.

My bread is your sustenance.
My heart is your heart. We are life.
My beauty is your beauty. I Am beauty.
My joy is your joy. I Am joy.

My skies are filled with My birds.
My oceans are filled with My fish.
My lands are filled with My trees.
My deserts are filled with My sands.

I Am in you.

I Am everywhere. I Am in everything.

I Am all Life.

I Am all space. I Am all time.

I Am eternal. I will never leave you or be destroyed, for I Am All There Is.

I Am in you. You are in Me.

Together we are One.

TOUCH AND YOU WILL FEEL ME

When you call, I Am The Answer.
When you are confused, I Am the question.

When you believe, I Am your miracle.
When you love, I Am your love.
When you feel, I Am your feeling.
When you create, I Am your opportunity.
When you are open, I Am your door.
When you give, I Am your riches.

When you think you have no more, I Am your abundance.
When you think you have no food, I Am your sustenance.

When you are parched, I Am your water.
When you are tired, I Am your strength.

When you dream, I Am your wonder.
When you believe, I Am your champion.
When you fear, I Am your warrior.

■■■

I do not destroy, only heal.

I know no suffering, only happiness.
I know no sadness, only gladness.
I know no lack, only abundance.
I know no pain, only love.

I know no weakness, only strength.
I know no cold, only warmth. I warm your heart.

I light your path for I Am The Way.

I Am All There Is.

I Am in you, you are in Me. Together we are One.

▪▪▪

Do not be afraid. Answer when I call.
Do not be confused. Follow Me when I guide.
Do not worry. I will protect you when you fear.

I Am beauty when you create, for I Am beauty.
I Am opportunity when you need, for I Am opportunity.
I Am love when you share from your soul, for I Am love.
I Am comfort when you cry, for I Am comfort.
I Am abundance when you lack, for I Am abundance.

I protect you from storms, for I Am the sun.

Have courage to dream, for I Am the stars.
Have faith to wonder, for I Am knowledge.
Have power to move, for I Am strength.

▪▪▪

Be still and you will hear Me.
Touch and you will feel Me.

Reach out and I will catch you.
Call My name and I will protect you.
Pray and I will provide clarity.

Sin and I will forgive you, but do not sin, for I Am only love. I am not sin.
Be afraid and I will guide you, but do not fear, for I Am only courage.

I will light your way. I will guide your steps.

I Am thanksgiving when you are glad.
I Am love when you open your heart.
I Am beauty when you open your eyes and see.

When you see, you see Me.
When you hear, you hear Me.
When you touch, you feel Me.

When you are angry, you do not hurt Me.

I love you. I Am here to guide you for I Am in you and I Am The Way.

I Am the path for your feet.
I Am the warmth for your cold.

I Am joy for your sadness.
I Am riches for your poverty.

I provide when you lack.

I create a way when you do not see a way, for I Am The Way.

▪▪▪

I Am willpower when you give up.
I Am success when you feel like failing.
I Am light when you are in darkness.
I Am strength when you are weak.
I Am happiness when you are sad.

I Am peace when you fear.
I Am love when you love.
I Am the overflow when you share.
I Am abundance when you create.
I Am power when you move.
I Am confidence when you believe.

I provide success when you struggle.
I provide riches when you are poor.
I provide healing when you are sick.

I comfort when you cry.

I laugh with you when you are joyful, for I Am joy.
I celebrate with you when you are thankful, for I Am happiness.
I create with you when you wonder, for I Am creation.
I guide you when you are lost, for I Am The Way.

■■■

I Am courage when you are weak. I Am strength.
I Am comfort when you hurt. I Am healing.

I astound when you dream. I Am wonder.

I Am courage when you believe. I Am eternity.

I Am The Answer when you question, for I Am All There Is.

I Am space. I Am time. I created space. I created time.
I Am love. I Am joy. I created love. I created joy.

I Am comfort when you are in pain. I Am your protection.

I Am waters when you thirst, for I Am the oceans. I Am in every wave.

■■■

My stars fill the sky. My trees fill the land.

My beauty provides you joy.

When you are weak, I will strengthen you.

When you cannot walk, I will carry you.
When you cannot stand, I will be your feet.
When you cannot hear, I will be your ears.
When you cannot see, I will be your eyes.

When you are confused, I will be your knowledge.
When you are weak, I will be your power.
When you are lost, I will be your guide.
When you are in danger, I Am your protection.

When you wonder, I Am your dreams.

■■■

You are My creation. I Am creation.
You are My love. I Am love.
You are My beauty. I Am beauty.

You are My joy. I Am joy.
You are My happiness. I Am happiness.
You are My miracles. I Am miraculous.
You are My overflow. I Am abundance.

You have time to do My work. I Am eternity.
You have strength to move. I Am strength.
You have courage to dream. I Am courage.
You have wonder to create. I Am wonder.

You have power to forgive. My power is in you. I Am your forgiveness.

You have plenty when you are thankful. I Am your provider.

You have music when you celebrate because I dance with you.

I Am your gladness.

■■■

I heal when you are sick, for I Am the cure.
I light when you are lost, for I Am the sun and the stars in the sky.

I Am the earth. I Am the moon. I Am the planets. I Am the galaxies.

I Am the small and the big, for I created the small and the big.
I Am the air and the seas, for I created the air and the seas.
I Am the birds and the trees, for I created the birds and the trees.
I Am the fish and the oceans, for I created the fish and the oceans.

My love is in you for I Am love.

I Am celebration when you dance.
I Am movement when you are stuck.
I Am guidance when you are lost.
I Am clarity when you are confused.

I Am The Answer before you ask the question, for I Am All There Is.

I Am in you. You are in Me.
Together we are One.

DO NOT HOLD BACK YOUR LOVE

Do not fear. I Am courage.
Do not cry. I Am comfort.
Do not destroy. I Am creation.
Do not argue. I Am peace.

Do not be confused. I Am knowledge.

Do not be afraid to dream. I Am wonder.
Do not be afraid to share. I Am your provider.
Do not be afraid to feel. I Am your heart.

Do not hold back your love. I Am your love.
I Am love. My love is in everyone, everywhere, in all eternity.

Do not be afraid to breathe. I Am your air.
Do not be afraid to move. I Am your path.

When you cannot walk, I will carry you.

When you cannot feel, I will give you the courage to feel.
When you cannot love, I will give you the courage to love.

I Am love.

My power is unlimited.
My possibility knows no bounds.
My skies have no endings.

I Am All There Is.

I Am in you. You are in Me.
Together we are One.

▪▪▪

Do not struggle, I Am strength.
Do not worry, I Am peace.
Do not confuse, I Am clarity.
Do not lack, I Am abundance.
Do not hurt, I Am forgiveness.
Do not be weary, I Am strength.
Do not hold back, I Am the overflow.

▪▪▪

Release and I will catch you.
Sleep and I will wake you.
Dream and I will astonish you.
Rise up and I will power you.
Question and I will answer you.

I Am The Answer before you ask the question.

I will provide before you lack.

I Am life when you want to die.

There is no death, only life.
There is no sadness, only joy.
There is no fear, only courage.
There is no darkness, only light.
There is no suffering, only love.

▪▪▪

When it seems like there is not, believe and I will amaze.
When it seems like all is lost, give and I will provide.
When it seems like dreams are unfulfilled, hope and I will create.
When it seems like life is broken, forgive and I will love. I Am love.
When it seems like there is sadness, be joyful for I Am joy.

When you think you feel pain, cry out and I will heal.

I hear your prayers when you call My name.

I catch you when you fall.
I see when you are blind.
I hear when you are deaf.

Where there is no way, I will make a way for I Am The Way.
When it seems there is no love, open your hearts, for I Am love.

I Am courage. I Am possibility.
I Am endless. I Am eternity.

I Am beginnings. There are no endings.
I Am limitless. There are no bounds.

When I heal, there is no more sickness.
When I amaze, there is no more doubt.
When I answer, there are no more questions, for I Am The Answer.

Do not give up, for I Am all possibility.
Do not hold back, for I Am all abundance.
Do not worry, for I Am all clarity.

When you look down, I will lift you up.
When you feel lost, do not fear, for I Am everywhere.

I Am in you. I Am All There Is.
You are in Me. Together we are One.

■■■

Where there are storms, I Am the rain.
Where there is light, I Am the sun.

When you breathe, I Am the air.
When you walk, I Am the earth.
When you look up, My stars signal that I Am here.
When you believe, My miracles cast aside all doubt.
When you stumble, I clear your path for I Am The Way.

I Am The Answer before you ask the question, for I Am knowledge.
I Am the clarity when you worry, for I Am clear.
I catch you when you fall, for My love runs deep.

BELIEVE, FOR I AM COURAGE

Be open and I will fill you. Be giving and I will love you.

When you are ready, I Am able. When you are not ready, I will teach you.

My lessons are here so you may understand My love.
My blessings are here so you may appreciate My bounty.

Your heart beats so you may know My life.
Your lungs fill with air so I breathe My life into you.

You love so you feel My love.

You dance so you may hear My music.
You move so you may explore My path.
You dream so you have courage to create.

When you sleep, I will wake you so you may do My work.
When you share, I will provide so you may experience My abundance.

▪▪▪

Be still for I Am with you.

Cry and I will wipe your tears.
Fear and I will encourage you.
Walk and I will move you.
Dream and I will inspire you.
Believe and I will amaze you.

My possibilities are endless.
My miracles are everywhere.

All of My creations are unique.
All of My creations are loved.
All of My creations are protected.
All of My creations are guided.

I Am The Way. I Am The Answer.

I Am the light in times of darkness.
I Am the power in times of weakness.
I Am the beauty in times of sadness.
I Am the overflow in times of abundance.
I Am the healing in times of sickness.
I Am the courage in times of fear.
I Am the love in times of hate.
I Am the peace in times of war.
I Am the clarity in times of confusion.
I Am the water in times of drought.
I Am the food in times of famine.

I see you when you do not see.
I hear you when you do not speak.
I listen when you do not cry.
I answer when you do not question.

▪▪▪

You do not have to do anything, for I Am everything.

I Am all creation. I Am all space. I Am in all time for I Am eternal.

My love is eternal. My joy is eternal. My beauty is eternal.

You are My masterpiece as you can receive My love, My joy and My beauty.

Do My work and I will provide you with My bounty.
Share My message and I will provide you with My love.

Celebrate My miracles and I will astonish your capacity to believe, for I Am limitless and My possibilities are endless.

I Am The Answer before you ask the question.

I Am your steps before you walk.
I Am your dreams before you wake.
I Am your insight before you create.

Fall and I will catch you.
Leap and I will fly with you.

Soar and I will fill My skies with love.
Swim and I will deepen My oceans with My living water.

Breathe in, for I Am the air.
Believe, for I Am courage.

Have faith, for I perform miracles.

Be bold, for you are unique and I Am creation.

Share, for I Am wealth.
Be joyful, for I Am beauty.
Receive, for I Am giving.

Listen to Me, for I hear you.
Open your eyes, for I see you.
Dare to dream, for I will wake you.

Be ready for I Am able.

■■■

Share My message. Share My love.

Open your gifts and hearts.

Believe and I will provide.
Hope and I will encourage.

Celebrate and you will know My joy.

When you open My doors, you will find My treasures.
When you are thankful, you will understand My gladness.
When you believe, you will experience My miracles.

Share My love and I will provide endless love.
Share My riches and I will provide eternal abundance.
Share My message and I will provide timeless answers.

Explore My path and I will offer limitless possibilities.

Soar in My skies and My stars will shine.

Walk across My lands and I will light your way.

I Am The Way. I Am The Answer.
I Am life. I Am love.

I Am in you. You are in Me.

Together we are One.

▪▪▪

Where you see an ending, I will make a new beginning.

When you are hungry, I will share the food from My table.
When you are discouraged, I will provide opportunity.
When you are sad, I will lift you with My joy.

When you dream, I will inspire you with My magic.

When you believe, My possibilities are endless.

My miracles will amaze and astound.

I Am in you. You are in Me.

Together we are One.

YOUR HEART IS MY HEART

God, I know You forgive me, as I always try my best.
God, I know You lift me, as I always feel your encouragement.
God, I know You love me, as I always feel your connection.

Your heart is my heart. Your love is my love.
Your knowledge is my answer to my question not yet asked.

You are always with me, as You are eternal and all powerful.
Your possibilities are endless as You are creation, and I am your work.

I am your servant. I answer your call.

I will share your message of hope.
I will speak boldly and You will provide the words to say.
I will believe and You will demonstrate your strength.

Lands will shake. Seas will roar.
But all eyes will look up at your miracles and capture your love.

I love You. You love me. Together we are One.

■■■

When I am imprisoned, You are my freedom.
When I am thirsty, You are my water.

When I am doubtful, You are my answer. You Are The Answer.
When I am lost, You light my way. You Are The Way.

When I am weak, You provide me with strength. You are strength.
When I lack, You share your riches. You are abundance.

Your opportunities are endless. Your possibilities are endless.

I believe in You. I am thankful You believe in me.
I love You. I celebrate your wonders.
I trust in You. I am in awe of your miracles.

I am always here with You, as I know You are always here with me.

You are eternal. You are everywhere, in everyone.
You are creation. You are my creator.
You forgive me. You are my savior.

I am yours. You are mine. Together we are One.

I travel your lands. I traverse your seas.

You conquer my enemies. You demonstrate your power.
Your magic awes. Your miracles amaze.
Your love makes me stronger.

I am in You. You are in me. Together we are One.

GOD NEEDS US

I am willing. I am able.

God is willing. God is able.

All things are possible when we believe.

God is all possibility. God Is All There Is.

God knows all. God sees all.
God knows us. God sees us.

"Help me see," we ask God and God helps us see.
"Free our minds from confusion," we ask, and God provides clarity.
"Show me what path I should walk," we ask, and God shows us The Way.

God is The Way.

God needs us just like we need God.

God's love powers us just as the earth revolves around the sun, and the moon around the Earth.

He is energy. He is light.
He is our strength.
He is our redemption from trouble.
He is our protector from evil.
He is our water when we thirst and our comfort when we cry.

▪▪▪

There are no limits because God is limitless.
There are no bounds because God is boundless.

God Is All There Is. We are One with God.

God needs us to do great things. God guides us to explore His path.

God loves us so we may open our hearts and share His love.

God's grace is everlasting. God is everlasting.

People question. God answers.
People have problems. God has solutions.

His creation is eternal. It never ends. God never ends.

His wonders are ceaseless.
His beauty is ageless.
His wishes are perfect and pure.

Love knows no bounds. Time and space have no ends.

God has the means to carry us, to deliver us, to encourage us, to protect us, to redeem us, to clothe us, to feed us, to quench our thirst, to light our way, to direct our steps, to lift us from anxiety, to relieve our worry, to answer our doubt, to calm our fears.

God is everywhere. God is in us. God Is All There Is.

▪▪▪

God is everlasting. We are everlasting.
God is ever joyful. We are His joy.

God's promises are always fulfilled. We are His promise.

God's medicine always cures. We need His healing.
God's forgiveness always redeems. We need His grace.

We are thankful for God. God is thankful for us.

When we trust in God, God trusts in us.

When we look up at the sun and the stars, we see God.
When we look into a baby's eyes, God sees us.
When we swim in God's oceans, we float on the waves of God.

■■■

God is pure energy.
God is pure love.
God is pure joy.
God is pure ecstasy.
God is pure courage.

God casts aside all doubt.
God heals all sickness.
God mends all broken wings and broken hearts.

We are His creations. Our success is His joy.

God can move mountains. He is our strength.
God can bring light from darkness. He is our light.

When God holds our hands, we are encouraged.
When God helps us to walk, we are lifted.

When we are moved, God is moved.
When we love, God shows His love.
When we forgive, God provides His grace.
When we believe, God delivers great miracles.
When we are quiet, God hears us.
When we are afraid, God comforts us.
When we wake from our dreams, God greets us with His possibility.

We can fly. God is our skies.
We can soar. God is our heavens.
We can rise up. God is our power.
We can believe. God is our provider.
We can be lifted. God is our encouragement.

Soldiers cry when they spill blood because all blood is God's blood.

God is life. God is inside of us.
We are inside of God.
Together, we are unstoppable.

▪▪▪

God demonstrates His magic every day.

His magic is in the love of a child.

It is in the innocence of youth.
It is in the beauty of nature.
It is in the waves in the oceans.
It is in the stars in the sky.

It is when we experience Heaven on Earth.
It is when we walk upright in confidence.
It is when we proclaim His might and give thanks.
It is when our hearts are pure and our mouths are fed.
It is when our pain ends because God is our relief.

God releases us from suffering.

He forgives us for our disbelief.
He rights our wrongs and erases our transgressions.

Believe in God for He always delivers. Look up to God and call out His name for He is always with us and always hears us.

He hears us when we cry.
He carries us when we stumble.
He answers when we call His name.

God is the answer to questions never asked.
God has miracles in store for us, for problems not yet conceived.

▪▪▪

Possibility is everywhere. God is everywhere. God is possibility.
Love is everywhere. God is everywhere. God is love.
Kindness is everywhere. God is everywhere. God is kindness.
Beauty is everywhere. God is everywhere. God is beauty.
Joy is everywhere. God is everywhere. God is joy.
Grace is everywhere. God is everywhere. God is grace.

Miracles abound when we believe in God.

God always believes in us.

He is our champion. He is our rock. He is our salvation.

God Is All There Is. and all there ever will be.

God's hands hold us.
God's feet move us.
God's courage strengthens us.
God's power energizes us.
God's air breathes life into us.
God's sun wakes us.
God's stars calm us.
God's path directs us.
God's joy lifts us.
God's miracles enthrall us.

God Is All There Is. We are One in God.
God is in all of us. We are all in God.
God's purity is in us. We are pure in God.
God's love is in us. We are love in God.
God's mercy is in us. We are mercy in God.
God's strength is in us. We are strength in God.
God's energy is in us. We are energy in God.

God needs us. We need God.

ALL PATHS LEAD TO ME

I Am God, calling you in your consciousness.
I Am God, inspiring you in your dreams.
I Am God, shielding you from your enemies.
I Am God, protecting you from your storms.
I Am God, forgiving you from your sins.
I Am God, loving you for your thanksgiving.
I Am God, trusting you for your faith.

I Am God, believing in you, for your belief in My possibilities.

My possibilities are endless.

Nothing is impossible in My mind.
Nothing is unstoppable from My strength.
Nothing is difficult for My magic.

My love is eternal. I Am eternal.
My grace is pure. I Am pure.
My creation is holy. I Am holy.

You are whole. You are worthy.

You have courage, for I Am your courage.

You have time, for I Am eternity.

■■■

Help is always at hand, for I Am always here.

I rise with you. I stand with you.
I walk with you. I run with you.

I Am peace. I Am beauty. I Am joy.

My hope triumphs over sadness.
My love conquers all evil.
My trust sustains all life.

■■■

I created all living things. I created you.

My creation is ongoing. Life is eternal.

I Am time, I Am space.
I Am wind, I Am rain.
I Am clouds, I Am sun.
I Am moon, I Am stars.

I Am possibility.

You are My possibility.

You are here to do great work and discover My magic and proclaim My message.

Answer when I call. I will never leave you.

Call and I will answer. I will never forsake you.

My promise is your happiness.
My knowledge is your clarity.
My heart is your peace.

I Am your possibility.

My possibility is endless.

My courage conquers your fear.
My magic demonstrates My power.

▪▪▪

Eternal life is yours when you believe.

I believe in you.

Believe in Me, and I will guide you.
Trust in Me, and I will comfort you.

Follow Me. Your unknown is My known.
See Me. Your blindness is My sight.
Love Me. Your prayer is always answered.

▪▪▪

I Am everywhere you look.

Where you see beauty, I Am there.
When you feel love, I Am in your heart.

Be open and I will fill you.
Be gracious and I will bless you.
Be kind and I will provide for you.
Be willing and I will be able.

I Am always able. I Am God.

You are in Me and I Am in you.

Together we are One.

▪▪▪

Hunger and I will feed you.
Hope and I will astound you.
Believe and I will amaze you.

Lose your way and I will deliver you.
Create and I will cherish you.
Fear and I will protect you.
Cry and I will encourage you.
Love and I will open you.

When you close, I will free you.

When you are challenged, I will lift your burdens.

▪▪▪

I Am The Way. All paths lead to Me.
I Am The Answer. All problems are solved by Me.
I Am The Light. All darkness is conquered by Me.
I Am Creation. All There Is, and all there will ever be, is made by Me.

▪▪▪

You are made in My image.
You are beautiful to Me.
Your dreams are My dreams.
Your power is My power.
Your wonder is My wonder.

Let Me demonstrate My miracles. I will astonish you.

Dare to explore. I will guide you.
Open your heart. I will love you.
Share My magic. I will amaze you.
Proclaim My word. I will fill you.
Create in My name. I will inspire you.
Call out My name. I will answer you.
Cry out in pain. I will comfort you.
Grow tired and falter, I will strengthen you.
Close your eyes and ears, I will encourage you.

I Am in you. You are in Me.

Together we are One.

▪▪▪

My skies have no limits.
My beginnings never end.
My beauty never fades.
My wonders never cease.
My magic never fails.
My creation never disappoints.
My power never wavers.

My message is truth.
My favor is pure.
My love is everlasting.

My beloved is you.

YOUR STRENGTH IS MY STRENGTH

I am thankful. I am in awe.

Your wonders amaze me.
Your words inspire me.
Your creation never ceases.
Your power never fails.
Your magic captivates me.
Your answers enlighten me.
Your love emboldens me.

I am free when I am in your arms.

I can soar in your skies of possibility.

I am clear. I am confident. I am led.

I am in You. You are in me.

For this I am thankful.

Together we are One.

■■■

You lift me when I fall.
You hear me when I cry.
You comfort me when I hurt.
You forgive me when I fail.
You catch me when I stumble.

You strengthen me when I am fragile.
You love me when I create.

Your joy is my joy.
Your beauty is my beauty.
Your health is my health.
Your strength is my strength.
Your life is my life.

You are in me. I am in You.

Together we are One.

GOD IS MOVEMENT

I have a tremendous gift that I am ready to share with the world.

I am bold in my giving and receiving.

God Is All There Is. I am one with God.

I am strong. I am willing. I am able.

God is ready. God is here with me right now.

God is in all living creatures, now, or that ever were, and whomever will be.

God hears my heart beat.

He moves with my breath. He is in still waters and troubled waters.

■■■

I have confidence because God is confidence.
I have love because God is love.
I have beauty because God is beauty.
I have joy because God is joy.

God is all around us. God is inside of us.

God is a wave of energy and light.

He is the thunder that roars.

He can move mountains and uproot trees.
He performs miracles and astounding acts of kindness.

Where mercy reigns, God reigns.
When hope prevails, God prevails.

God births galaxies and stars. He orders the orbits of planets and moons.
He works as the light of the sun and can be seen in the darkness of night.

He is ever present, always available.
He needs us as we need Him.
He is everywhere and in everyone.

We are all One.

God Is All There Is.

Together we are One.

▪▪▪

God is hope. God is abundance.
God is laughter to wipe away tears.
God is joy to overcome sadness.
God is health to conquer sickness.
God is righteousness to destroy wickedness.

God brings beauty to darkness.
God brings healing to suffering.
God brings quiet to noise.

God is energy. God is movement.

God moves whether we see Him or not.

God is conscious of us whether we are conscious of Him or not.

God is the sun in the morning and the stars at night.

God wakes us from our dreams with His unlimited possibility.

God is All There Is. We are One in God.

NO PROBLEM IS TOO BIG FOR ME

You are created in My likeness and image.
You are My pride and joy.

I will deliver you from evil.
I will right your wrongs.
I will heal your wounds.
I will forgive your suffering.

I will bring gladness to all of your days and inspiration and courage when you dream at night.

When you wake, I Am here, ready and able.

I will carry you. I will support you.

I always support you.
I always love you.
I always hear you.
I always see you, even when you do not see Me.

I comfort you when you hurt or not. I laugh with you when you feel My joy, and cry with you when you are in pain.

I will destroy your pain and perform great miracles.

I will demonstrate My wonder and awe, to embolden your power to believe, and ability to spread My word and My message.

My message is opportunity.
My message is favor.
My message is thanksgiving.
My message is hope.
My message is beauty.
My message is eternal.

I Am eternity.

I Am The Way. All paths lead to Me.
I Am the Answer. All problems are solved by Me.

I Am the light. I Am the sun. I Am the stars.
I Am the waters. I Am the lands.
I Am the earth beneath your feet and your steps that move you.

I hear your prayers. I hear your cries. I will not forsake you.

I love you. I Am All There Is.

I Am in everyone.

I Am God.

■■■

Fish swim in My oceans, and birds traverse My skies.

My skies are filled with My love and endless possibilities.
My lands are covered by My magic and My beauty.

Humanity is My greatest creation because you can appreciate My bounty and create in My name.

Create and I will provide you more riches than the stars in the sky. You will know happiness. You will know joy. You will know Me.

I know you. I created you. I created all.

I Am All There Is. I Am God.
You are in Me and I Am in you.

Together we are One.

■■■

Love one another and all will possess My love.

Be kind to one another and all will experience My kindness.
Be merciful to one another and all will share in My mercy.

No problem is too big for Me.
No prayer is too small for Me.
No wish is too impossible for Me.

I Am possibility.
I Am endless tomorrows.

I Am the brightness of day and the light that warms you.
I Am the coolness of night and the wind that comforts you.

I Am comfort. I Am joy.
I Am perfect. I Am complete.

I Am All There Is.

You are in Me. I Am in you.

You are whole.

You are an eternal being for I created you in My likeness and image and I Am eternity.

■■■

I Am love when you hate. I Am clarity when you stumble.

You shall never be lost, as all paths lead to Me, as I Am The Way.

Where there is no hope, believe and I will provide hope.
Where doors are closed, believe and I will open doors.

I will build bridges where there are no bridges.
I will compose music where there is no dancing.

I dance with you. I sing with you. I celebrate with you.

I Am glad when you are glad.

I rise with you when you stand.
I move with you when you walk.
I comfort you when you cry.
I wipe your tears when you are sad.

I will give you beauty for your sadness, and demonstrate My awe and wonder.

I Am all possibility. I Am all time and space.
I created time and space. I created all. I created you.

I Am All There Is.
You are in Me and I Am in you.

Together we are One.

▪▪▪

Love is all there is for I Am All There Is.
Mercy is all there is. Kindness is all there is.
I Am mercy. I Am kindness.

My power conquers weakness.
My wonders inspire. My beauty is everlasting.

You are everlasting. You are My joy.

I love you. I Am love.
I Am in you. You are in Me.

Together we are One.

DREAM, FOR MY CREATION NEVER ENDS

I will fill your openness.

Your cup will overflow when you drink My living water.
You will never be hungry when you eat My bread.
You are always welcome at My table.

I hear you always. I love you always. I provide always.

My magic never expires.
My wonders amaze.
My possibilities are your beliefs.
My knowledge is your questions.
My answers are timeless. I Am timeless.

I Am The Answer now and always.
I Am All There Is, all there ever was, and all there will ever be.

■■■

You swim in My oceans filled with love.
You dream in My nights full of joy.
You celebrate when you dance to My music.

Believe and you will see Me. I always see you. I Am in you. You are in Me.

Love and you will share Me.
Give and I will enrich you.
Move and I will embolden you.

Have courage for your power is My power.

Be merciful for your mercy is My mercy.
Be hopeful for your hope is My hope.

I Am alive. I Am life.
I Am celebration. I Am love.
I Am miracles. I Am possibility.

▪▪▪

Nothing is impossible for Me.

All problems are solved by Me, as I Am The Answer.

I Am timeless truth and eternal abundance.

I Am thanksgiving when you are thankful. I Am thankful.

When you are glad, I Am gladness.
When you are joyful, I Am joyous.
When you are fearless, I Am boundless.

I begin and never end. My wonders never cease.

I Am all time and space. I created time and space.

I created love. I Am love.
I created opportunity. I Am opportunity.

I Am energy. I Am light.
I Am the stars. I Am the skies.
I Am the earth. I Am the oceans.
I Am the lands. I Am the trees.

▪▪▪

My warmth inspires you and My forgiveness cools you.

My joy celebrates with you.
My possibilities dream with you.
My miracles awaken with you.

My love carries you. I Am love.
My beauty inspires you. I Am beauty.
My courage powers you. I Am courage.
My mercy forgives your sins. I Am mercy.
My kindness rights all wrongs. I Am kindness.
My possibilities are endless. I Am endless.

■■■

I conquer fear. I conquer death. There is no death, only life. I Am life.

I provide opportunity. I provide love. I Am opportunity. I Am love.

I cure all sickness. I heal all wounds. I banish all suffering.

I perform miracles. I move mountains.

I Am eternal. You are eternal.

You are My pride and joy.

I love you always. My love never ends. I never end.

I Am God.

I Am in you and you are in Me.

Together we are One.

■■■

You are priceless beyond measure.
You are beauty beyond compare.

You are unique.

You are powerful for I Am creation and provide your power.

My love breathes life into you. I Am the air.
My blood rushes through you. I Am the beating of your heart.

I Am in you. You are in Me. We are One, now and forever, in all time and space, for I Am time and space.

■■■

Your dreams are not too big for Me. Nothing is too big for Me.
Your courage is not too small for Me. Nothing is too small for Me.

Soar in My skies. I will lift you.
Travel across My lands. I will lead you.
Swim in My oceans. I will power you.
Rise up and I will strengthen you.
Walk and I will move you.
Believe and I will astonish you.

I amaze. I Am wonder. I Am awe.
I create. I Am beauty.
I celebrate. I Am joy.
I forgive. I Am kindness.

My miracles cure your sickness.
My water quenches your thirst.
My food satisfies your hunger.

Your joy feeds Me.
Your love feels Me.
Your thankfulness gladdens Me.
Your prayers warm Me.

Let Me demonstrate My miracles and awe.
Let Me embolden your belief and astonish your trust.

■■■

I Am beauty. I Am life.

Beauty is all there is. Life is all there is. I Am All There Is.

I Am kindness. I Am joy.

Kindness is all there is. Joy is all there is. I Am All There Is.

I Am the energy inside you.

My possibility is inside you.
My love and My hope is inside you.

Be loving. Be hopeful for I Am love and hope.

Believe, for My wonders never cease.
Dream, for My creation never ends.

Move for My power is endless and My energy boundless.

I Am timeless. I Am All There Is.

I Am eternity. You are eternal.

You are made in My likeness and image.

For this be thankful, for I created you.
For this be joyful, for I celebrate you.
For this be happy, for I sing with you.
For this be bold, for I dance with you.
For this be merciful, for I forgive you.

I forgive when you do not believe.
I hear you when you cry. I heal you when you hurt.
I will clear your path for I Am The Way.

All paths lead to Me, for I Am All There Is.

You are in Me and I Am in you.

Together we are One.

YOU ARE ETERNAL, I AM ETERNITY

I Am God.
I Am love. I Am hope. I Am light.

I Am quiet in the noise.
I Am silence in the storms.
I Am possibility where you see no possibility.

I make a way where there is no way. I Am The Way.

You are in Me. I Am in you.
Together we are One.

▪▪▪

Where mercy reigns, I reign. Where sickness destroys, I heal.

My beauty never fades. My wonders never end. I never end.

I Am boundless possibility and ceaseless creation.
I Am eternal love and amazing magic.
I Am astonishing joy and endless tomorrows.

You are eternal. You are My beloved.

I Am eternity. I Am All There Is.
I Am in you and you are in Me.

Together we are One.

■■■

I hear you when others do not hear.
I see you when others do not see.
I feed you when you hunger.
I comfort you when you cry.
I hold you when you fall.
I love you when you hate.

When you are blind, I will light your path.
When you are deaf, I will answer your prayers.

I Am The Answer to questions never asked.
I Am The Way where there are no paths.

I Am beauty where there is love and hope where there is belief.

Believe in Me. I believe in you.
Love Me. I love you. I Am love.

Pray and I will not forsake you.
Have courage and I will not disappoint you.

Swim in My oceans and I will not let you drown.
Walk on My earth and you will never be lost.
Soar in My skies and My power will lift you.
Look up at My stars and My energy will encourage you.

Celebrate My possibility. I celebrate you.
I Am celebration. I Am possibility.

Be joyful for Me. I Am joyful for you. I Am joy.
Be thankful for me. I Am thankful for you. I Am thanksgiving.

I Am Creation. I Am All There Is.
You are in Me and I Am in you.

■■■

You are eternal. I Am eternity.

There is no death, only life. I Am life.
There are no endings, only possibilities. I Am possibility.

There is no suffering, only mercy. I Am mercy.
There are no boundaries, only opportunities. I Am opportunity.
There are ceaseless tomorrows and timeless answers.
There is wonder and amazement.

I Am beauty. I Am awe.
I Am earth. I Am sky.
I Am planets. I Am stars.
I Am suns. I Am moons.

I Am in you. You are in Me.
Together we are One.

▪▪▪

Be kindness, for I Am kind.
Be loving, for I Am love.
Be forgiving, for I Am grace.
Be thankful, for I Am possibility.

Believe, for I Am opportunity.

Have courage to dream, for I Am your inspiration.
Have capacity to share, for I Am your provider.

Be bold for I created you in My likeness and image.
Be faithful for I believe in you. I created you. I Am creation.

I love you. You are My beloved.
I Am All There Is.
Together we are One.

▪▪▪

Have courage. I will lift you when you fall.
Have faith. I will comfort you when you cry.

Know My truth for I Am The Answer.
Seek My path for I Am The Way.
Look up at My sky for I Am The Light.
Create in My name for I Am Creation.

You are mine and I Am yours.
Together we are One.

YOUR LOVE IN ME IS MY JOY

Dear God:

Light my way. Direct my steps.
Hear my cries. See my possibility.

I am your possibility for You are possibility.

I do your work, for You created me. You are creation.

You answer me, for You are truth.
You power me, for You are courage.
You inspire me, for You are wonder.
You strengthen me, for You are might.
You provide for me, for You are abundance.
You love me, for You are forgiveness.
You lift me, for You are the air.
You fill my lungs, for You are my breath.
You clear my path, for You are The Way.

I know I am in You.

You know me for You created me. You are creation.
Your joy is in me for You celebrate with me. You are celebration.

I dance to your music.

I love for your love is in my heart.
I believe for your possibility is in my dreams.

I am thankful for I am in You, and You are in me.

Together we are unstoppable.
Together we are One.

▪▪▪

You catch me when I fall.
You answer when I question.
You encourage when I doubt.
You provide when I lack.
You amaze when I believe.
You deliver when I seek.
You forgive when I sin.
You correct when I stumble.
You comfort when I cry.
You hear me when I call your name.

I am thankful for you created me in your likeness and image.

Your beauty is in me.
Your wonder is everywhere.
Your possibility is endless.
Your love is boundless.
Your energy is ceaseless.
You are in me. You power me.

I am in You.
You are All There Is.
Together we are One.

▪▪▪

Your living water flows through me.
Your blood beats my heart and provides me life.

Your belief in me is my courage.
Your power in me is my strength.
Your love in me is my joy.

You are in me. I am in You.
Together we are One.

ALL OF GOD IS WITH US

I need to be humble. I need to be thankful.

God Is All There Is.

God created me.

God needs me.
God needs me to do His work.
God needs me to complete His love.
God needs me to speak of His wonders.
God needs me to deliver His miracles.
God needs me to share His grace.
God needs me to spread His beauty and kindness.
God needs me to walk upright on His path.
God needs me to glow in His light and wonder at His mercy.

■■■

Just as there are countless stars in the sky, there are countless wonders on Earth. God's wonders never cease. His miracles always amaze.

God's power is endless. His possibilities are boundless.

God's love is everywhere. God is everywhere. God is love.
God's beauty is everywhere. God is everywhere. God is beauty.
God's joy is everywhere. God is everywhere. God is joy.

God is All There Is. We are One in God.

▪▪▪

God directs my steps and lights my path. God Is The Way.

I am an open channel to receive and share God's mercy and love.
I will walk on God's path. Every path is His path.

God is everywhere and in everyone.

God is in me. God created me.

God created everything and everyone.
God loves everything and everyone.

When we are thankful for God, His love surrounds us.
His beauty inspires us.. His joy encourages us.
His mercy washes over us. His sun and stars shine bright.

Day and night, Heaven is near, God is here.

Love is here. Beauty is here.
Joy is here. Wonder is here.
Abundance is here. Power is here.

All of God is with us.
God is in us. God made us.
God made everything and everyone.

God Is All There Is. We are One in God.

God's mercy rains down on us.
God's knowledge feeds us.
God's kindness holds us.
God's love warms us.
God's power moves us.
God's possibilities lift us.
God's strength restores us.

God is endless.

We are eternal. God is Eternity.

God Is All There Is. We are One in God.

YOU ARE BEAUTIFUL TO ME

I Am God.

I Am always here for you. I Am always here with you.

I stand with you. I encourage you.
I deliver you from evil. I clear boundaries.

My love is boundless.
My power is ceaseless.
My creation is endless.

You are My creation.

I created you in My likeness and image.

You are beautiful to Me.

There are no wrongs, only rights in My eyes.
I can turn your wrongs into rights through My love and mercy.

Be thankful for Me. I Am thankful for you.
Be joyful for Me. I Am joyful for you.
Be loving for Me. I always love you.

I created you.

I created Heaven and Earth.
I birthed mountains and rivers.

I shine sun and stars.

My light warms your earth.
My heaven is filled with love.

▪▪▪

Beauty is everywhere. I Am everywhere. I Am beauty.
Love is everywhere. I Am everywhere. I Am love.
Mercy is everywhere. I Am everywhere. I Am mercy.
Abundance is everywhere. I Am everywhere. I Am abundance.

I give you everything you need so you may share My generosity.

I direct your steps and comfort your fears so you will lead others on My path and be encouraged to live boldly.

▪▪▪

You are unique. I Am Creation.
You have purpose. I Am your purpose.

My work needs completion.
My love needs to be shared.

My message needs to be delivered.

My message is hope in times of fear.
My message is thanksgiving and grace.

My message is beauty in times of darkness and wonders in times of sadness.

My message triumphs over evil and washes away sin and suffering.

I do not want you to suffer. I Am not suffering.
I do not want you to fear. I Am not fear.

Fear not. Suffer not.
Love always. Share always.

Respect everything. Be generous.
Live boldly. Dream wildly.

■■■

Discover greatness.

You are greatness.

My greatness is in you because I Am greatness and I Am in you.

See greatness in everyone. See beauty in everything.

Hear My voice. I hear you always.

Answer when I call. I answer you always.

■■■

Be loving.

Open your heart. I love you always.

My heart expands when you open your heart and share My love.

Share from your heart. Share from your soul. Share of yourself.

I Am in you. I Am your provider. I ensure you always have plenty.

Your happiness is My happiness. Your dreams are My dreams.

■■■

Live inspired.

Create in My name.
Dance to My music.
Discover My lands.
Soar in My skies.
Reach for My stars.

Nothing is too big for Me when you believe.
Nothing is too amazing for Me when you trust.

Opportunity is everywhere. Possibility is everywhere.
I Am opportunity. I Am possibility.

You are beautiful to Me.

I Am God. My beauty is in you.

I Am in you. You are in Me.

Together we are One.

▪▪▪

Love one another just as I love you.

Spread peace. Show faith. Share joy.

I will make your dreams come true. I Am truth.
I will open doors and unlock hearts. I Am The Way.
I will light your way. I Am your confidence.

Be open. Be available.
I Am always available. I never leave you.

When it seems like I Am not here, I Am here.
When it seems like I do not hear, I do hear.

I listen. I comfort you. I power you.

I lift you when you are weak.
I carry you when you cannot walk.
I inspire you when you open your eyes.
I sing with you when you share from your heart.

Where boldness reigns, I reign.
Where creativity blooms, I create.
Where storms subside, I calm.

I Am peace. I Am beauty. I Am love.
I Am the joy in your heart.

Your joy is My joy. I Am joy.

I Am God.

Together we are One.

WE GROW IN YOUR PRESENCE

I dance in your light. Your music moves me. Your words lift me.

My spirit soars in your Presence. Your Presence is in me, always with me.

I am clear. I am confident. I am led.

My steps are ordered before me.
You are creating the path for my feet.
You are moving mountains, clearing my way.

You are The Way. You are All There Is.

I am thankful you have blessed me.
I am honored you have chosen me.

You created me. You created all.
You created moon and stars.
You created galaxies and planets.

You are the leaves and the trees. We are your branches.

Your roots run deep. Your water sustains us.
Your fertile soil delivers our growth.

We grow in your Presence.
Your Presence is in us. We are in You.
You are All There Is. We are eternal.
You are in us.

LET YOUR IMAGINATION RUN WILD

I Am God.

Listen when I speak.
See when I provide.
Believe when I astonish.
Praise when I transform.

Honor My courage. Love My wonders.
I give you courage. I give you love.

Soar in My skies. My skies are filled with love.
Swim in My oceans. My waters overflow with peace.

▪▪▪

I Am joy. I Am happiness.
I Am day. I Am night.

I Am All There Is.

All you see, all you hear is from Me.
All you touch, all you dream is from Me.

You are from Me.

I Am in you. I created you.

I created you so you can feel My love.

I created you so you are moved by My power.
I created you so you are energized by My light.

I Am The Light. I Am The Way.

I Am God.

Surrender and I will protect you.
Call out My name and I will hear you.
Follow My path and I will guide you.
Share My hope and I will love you.

I always love you. I Am love.
My love is in you. I Am in you.
You are in Me. Together we are One.

▪▪▪

Be open. Be available. Answer when I call.

Dare to wonder and I will amaze.

Believe in My miracles and I will not disappoint.
I can not, I will not disappoint.

I Am All There Is.

I provide for you. I believe in you.

Believe in Me. Hear Me. See Me everywhere and in everyone.

I Am All There Is, and ever was, now and will ever be.

Time has no limits. I Am eternal. You are eternal.

My magic has no ends. I Am powerful. You are powerful.
My love has no walls. I Am courage. You are courageous.

When I lead, follow.
Lead others and I will guide you.
Speak of My beauty and I will inspire you.

Dare to dream. Dare to love.
Dare to hope. Dare to soar.

Dare to fly. I Am the air.
Dare to discover. I Am wonder and awe.

My miracles are awesome. You are awesome.

I created you. I created all.

You are My miracle.

Be bold, be brave.

Stumble and I will catch you.
Question and I will answer you.
Wonder and I will astonish you.
Dream and I will provide for you.

I always provide.
I Am All There Is.

We are One.

▪▪▪

Do My work and I will provide abundance. I Am abundance.
Speak My word and I will inspire you with My truth. I Am truth.
Love one another and I will give you the courage to love. I Am love.

Share My abundance. Share My truth. Share My love.
Give away My riches and I will provide more riches.

Rise up from your dreams.
Let your imagination run wild.
I power your dreams. I Am your inspiration.

You inspire Me when you walk My earth and marvel at My stars.

I created you in My likeness and image so you may share My beauty, wonder and awe. I Am wonder. I Am awe.

I Am God.
I Am All There Is.

Together we are One.

■■■

Have courage to fly. I Am the sky.
Have courage to soar. I Am the air.
Have courage to lead. I Am your guide.

I Am The Way. I Am on your path and directing your steps.

Follow Me and you will never be lost.
Believe in Me and you will never be confused.
Share My love and you will know no suffering. I am not suffering.
Celebrate My joy and you will know true freedom.
I Am celebration. I Am joy. I Am freedom.

I Am the Answer before you ask the question.

I Am your dream before you wake.

I sustain you. Be fully alive.

Walk My path and you will never be lost.
Swim My oceans and you will never drown.

Jump and you will not fall.

Believe and I will not fail. I never fail.

I Am All There Is. I Am God.

Together we are One.

WE ARE ENERGIZED BY GOD'S LOVE

God is here with me. God never leaves me.

God is in me. I am in God.

We are here together. We are never apart.

We are One. We are all in God.

God is in all.
God is in all of us.

God needs us. We need God.
God loves us. We love God.

God believes in us. We believe in God.
God astonishes us. We are amazed by God.
God provides for us. We are sustained by God.
God created us. We create in the name of God.

When we call out, God hears us.
When we cry out, God comforts us.
When we cannot move, God carries us.
When we cannot feel, God inspires us.

God powers our dreams. God orders our steps.

God creates a path where there is no path.

God Is The Way. All paths lead to God.

God Is All There Is.

I am thankful.

Together we are One.

■■■

God is grace. God is courage.
God heals. God amazes.
God loves. God astounds.

God is boundless. God is energy.

We are energized by God's love.
We are healed by God's presence.

God's power moves us.
God's courage wakes us.
God's grace forgives us.

We are forgiven. God is love.
We are unique. God is creation.

God is beauty. We are beautiful.
God is wonder. We are wonderful.
God is magic. We are magical.

God transforms us.

God is in the young and the old.

God is in all. All are in God.

Together we are One.

LEAP AND FLY WITH ME

I Am God, calling out to you.

Call out to Me and I answer your prayers.

Ask and I provide. Open and I forgive.

Love and I will be your love. I Am love.
Create and I will be your beauty. I Am beauty.
Celebrate and I will be your joy. I Am joy.

Be ready and I will be able. I Am always able.
I Am always with you. I Am always in you.

You are always in Me. Together we are One.

▪▪▪

Let Me in and I will astonish you.
Share My magic and I will amaze you.
Proclaim My miracles and I will power you.

Leap and fly with Me.
Jump and move with Me.
Dream and create with Me.

I Am creation. I created all. I created you.
I Am in you. You are in Me.
Together we are One.

▪▪▪

Love one another. I Am in everyone.
Forgive one another. I forgive everyone.
Dance with one another. I celebrate everyone.

Be bold. Be loving. I Am your boldness. I Am your love.

I Am time. I Am space.
I Am wind. I Am rain.
I Am earth. I Am sun.
I Am day. I Am night.
I Am sky. I Am land.

I Am the fish in the seas and the leaves on the trees.
I Am the sands in the deserts and the pebbles on the shore.

I Am your rock. Follow Me and you will never be lost.
I Am your shield. I Am your freedom.

I heal. I transform.
I amaze. I Am awe.
I astonish. I Am power.
I forgive. I Am redemption.
I redeem. I Am your provider.
I create. I Am your creator.

I created all.

I Am All There Is.

I Am God.

FOR THIS I AM THANKFUL

I am open. I am your channel. I am your vessel.

Use me. Hear me. Heal me.
Transform me. Redeem me. Forgive me.

I am forgiven. You forgive all.
I am loved. You love all.

I am held in your arms. You carry all.
I am lifted by your possibility. You inspire all.

You are All There Is.

I am in You. You are in me.
Together we are One.

▪▪▪

I am in direct contact with the Divine.

You are divine. Your divinity is in me.

You feel my feelings.
You right my wrongs.
You order my steps.
You forgive my sins.

I am transformed. I am healed.

I am loved. You are love.
I am courageous. You are courage.

I am joyful. You are my joy. I am your joy.

For this I am thankful.
You are in me. I am in You.

Together we are One.

■■■

Heaven is at hand. You are always at hand.
Your hand moves the waters. Your love is living water.

My happiness is your happiness. You are happiness.
My peace is your peace. You are peace.
You are time. You are space. You are All There Is.

We are in You. You are in us.

We are thankful.

Together we are One.

GOD IS EVERYWHERE

God is everywhere.

Everywhere we are, God Is.

God is the future. God is the now.
God is all there ever was and all will be.

God cares for us when man does not care.
God provides for us. No one else can.

God holds our hearts in His hands.
God holds our dreams. He is our inspiration.

We are His joy. We are His passion.

Our passion is fueled by God. His love fuels our fire.

His mercy fulfills our desires.

Where mercy reigns, God reigns.

God quenches our thirst.

He orders our steps.
He answers our questions.
He hears our prayers.
He heals our pain.
He solves our problems.

He wipes our tears.

He leaps with us. He soars with us.
He stands with us on solid ground.

■■■

God is everywhere and in everyone.

He created all.

He loves all of His creations.
He wants us to receive His abundance.
He longs to fulfill our wishes.

His joy comes when we dream and when we wake.

He directs us when we are lost. God Is The Way.

He forgives us when we fail.
He wipes our tears when we hurt. God Is The Answer.

He shines His light when we stumble in darkness. God Is The Light.
He answers our questions when we are confused. God Is truth.
He provides solutions when we are blind. God Is opportunity.
He dances with us when we sing His song. God Is bliss.
He inspires us when we dream. God Is possibility.

All things are possible in the mind of God.
All love is possible in the heart of God.

Our hearts overflow with God's love.

His magic is in the air..
His miracles fill the skies.

He is all space and all time.

God is eternal. We are eternal.

We live inside God's eternity.

Together we are One.

ALL THINGS ARE MADE NEW TODAY

I Am God, reaching out to you.

Take My hand and I will show you the way. I Am The Way.

I will inspire you so you may inspire others.
I will instruct you so you may teach others.

I will be happy with you so you may share My joy.
I will create for you so you may speak of My magic.
I will demonstrate My wonder for you so you may deliver My message.

My message is hope.
My message is endless favor.
My message is eternal tomorrows.

All things are made new today.
All chaos is made ordered today.
All dreams are coming true today.
All opportunities are possible today.
All miracles are made real today.
All creation is made beautiful today.
All sins are washed clean today.
All pasts are forgiven today.
All wrongs are made right today.
All sickness is healed by My power today.
All energy is made manifest by My light today.
All paths are made clear by My truth today.

I Am truth. I Am love. I Am joy.
I Am wisdom. I Am creation.

I created you. I created all.

I Am All There Is.

I Am all there was. I Am all there will ever be.

I do not begin. I never end. I Am limitless.

I Am all space and time.
I Am all stars and galaxies.
I Am all heaven and earth.
I Am all the leaves on all the trees.
I Am all the sand on every shore.

My wind carries you across My oceans.
My wings allow you to fly in My skies.
My miracles exist to provide you with My hope.

Believe and you will see.
Cry out and I will hear.
Stumble and I will catch you.
Leap and I will fly with you.
Dream and I will inspire you.
Create and I will be your beauty.
Celebrate and I will be your joy.

Lack and I will provide you with plenty.
Sleep and I will wake you with My possibility.
Fall and I will lift you with My opportunity.

I Am opportunity. I Am wisdom.

I Am eternal. You are eternal.

We live and move and breathe in eternity.

LIFE IS MAGICAL, LOVE IS POWERFUL

I Am All There Is.

Everything I have, you are.

My magic is inside of you.
My love is inside of you.
My courage is inside of you.

Do not despair for I Am near.
Do not worry for I Am always here.
Do not fear for I always provide.

Do not destroy for I always create. I Am creation.
Do not be confused for I always answer. I Am The Answer for questions not yet asked.

Do not grow hungry for I always sustain.
Do not cry for I always comfort.
Do not be anxious for I always calm.

I Am God. I Am everywhere.

Wherever I Am, you are. Wherever you are, I Am.

Know that I Am always with you.
Know that My possibility is always inside of you.
Know that My beauty always creates with you.

▪▪▪

Life is magical. Love is powerful.

Today is made for your dreams to come true. I Am truth.
Tomorrow is near for My power to amaze. I Am wonder and awe.

The past exists so you may learn My lessons. I Am The Answer.

My path is in front of you so you may never be lost. I Am The Way.

All paths lead to Me.
All dreams wake with Me.
All prayers are answered by Me.
All problems are solved by Me.
All wishes are fulfilled by Me.
All sins are washed away by Me.
All love is made real by Me.

All hearts expand with My love.
All hearts beat with My eternal forgiveness.

All lungs fill with My air. Your breath is My breath.

All hands create with My wonder.

Your creation is My creation. I Am creation.

All dreams are made manifest by My power.

I Am energy. I Am light.

I Am truth. You are true. Life is true.
I Am love. You are loved. Love is real.

I Am possibility. Believe in My possibility.

All things are possible because I created all.

▪▪▪

I Am space. I Am time.
I Am wind. I Am rain.
I Am sun. I Am sky.

I Am all the water in all the oceans.
I Am everything there is and will ever be.

All I have, you are.

You are inside of Me. I Am inside of you.

Together we are One.

▪▪▪

You can see with My eyes.
You can hear with My ears.
You can love with My heart.
You can forgive with My truth.
You can dream with My peace.
You can celebrate with My joy.
You can believe with My hope.
You can journey with My possibility.

Walk on My path. I Am The Way.
Answer when I call. I Am The Answer.
Forgive where there is darkness. I Am The Light.
Believe and I will amaze. I Am Creation.

I Am God.

Together we are One.

▪▪▪

Your possibility is My possibility.
Your joy is My joy.
Your courage is My courage.
Your love is My love.

Believe in Me. I believe in you.
Celebrate with Me. I celebrate you.
Laugh with Me. I Am glad with you.
Sing with Me. I will dance with you.
Pray with Me. I will answer you.

When you hunger, I will feed you.
When you thirst, I will sustain you.

When you believe, I will amaze and astound you.

I Am wonder. I Am awe.

All things are possible. I Am all possibility. I Am all.

Everything I Am is already in you.

You are always in Me. I Am always in you.

Together we are One.

▪▪▪

Celebrate My miracles and I will provide more miracles.
Be inspired by My dreams and I will wake you with My love.
Believe in My magic and I will move mountains for you.

Swim in My oceans and you will never drown.
Soar in My skies and you will never fall.

Believe in My possibility and I will never disappoint.

Walk across My lands and you will never be lost.
Reach for My hand and you will never be alone.

▪▪▪

Have courage. It is already inside of you.
Give love. Your heart expands with My love.
Spread joy. Your happiness is made real by Me.
Share abundance. Your wealth is created by Me.
Be thankful. Everything you have and all that you are is given by Me.

I have given you the world.

You are My world. You are My pride and joy.

I created you so you may speak of Me and encourage others.

I love you. I always love you.

I Am God.
Together we are One.

■■■

Your happiness is My happiness.
Your joy is My joy.
Your creation is My creation.

You are My miracle.

Celebrate all of My miracles.
Believe in all of My possibilities.

My powers are endless.
My wonders never cease.
My heart always forgives.

Sit at My table and I will feed you.
Speak of My magic and I will bless you.

Look up in the skies. You will see Me in the stars.

I Am the sun. I Am the moon.
I Am the planets. I Am the galaxies.
I Am all space. I Am all time.

Everything I have, you are.

I Am in you. You are in Me.

Together we are One.

I Am God. I Am All There Is.

Together we are complete.

THANK YOU

Thank you God for all you have given me.

You bless me. You forgive me.
You hear me. You see me.
You right my wrongs.
You heal my wounds.
You answer my confusion
You provide when I need.

I am thankful for You. I am thankful for all.

Together we are One.

I DELIVER ON MY PROMISES

I Am here with you. I Am always here with you.
I Am eternal. I do not begin or end. I Am All There Is.

You are a part of Me. I created you.

We are One and the same, connected always.

I love you always. I Am love.
I care for you always. I Am compassion.
I heal your pain always. I Am kindness.
I dry your tears always. I Am comfort.

I know you always.
I hear you always.
I celebrate you always.
I forgive you always.

I Am always here, ready and able to provide you with more abundance than you can conceive.

Let your imagination run wild.
Your dreams are My dreams.

I catch you when you fall.
I forgive you when you fail.
I champion you when you rise.
I celebrate you when you succeed.

Trust in Me. I cannot fail.
Believe in Me. I always amaze.
Fly with Me. Together we will soar.

▪▪▪

Everything I Am, you are:

The stars in the sky, the moon and the sun, the oceans and the waves.

Be courageous. You have courage. I Am courage.

Live boldly. Be fearless.

I conquer fear as My light conquers darkness. I Am light.

Question and I will answer. I Am The Answer for questions not yet asked.
Love and I will deliver. I Am the love in your heart. I Am love.

My promise is eternal. You are eternal.

I Am eternity. I do not begin and I never end.

I Am limitless. I Am boundless.
I Am power. I Am awe.
I Am wisdom. I Am truth.

Share My message. Share My hope.

I will give you the words to say when you have no words.
I will open doors where there are no doors.
I will open hearts when hearts are closed.
I will carry you. You cannot fail.

I Am All There Is.

Everything I Am, you are, because I made you and I Am in you.

You are in Me.

▪▪▪

My message is endless favor.
My message is timeless wonder.

My message is boundless possibility.
My message is limitless courage.
My message is eternal life.
My message is pure love.
My message is awesome joy.
My message is ecstatic bliss.
My message is powerful miracles.

My message is you.

You are the light in My eye. You are My beloved.

Deliver My message. Share My love.

My gifts are for you, and for everyone.

I Am All There Is.

Together we are One.

■■■

My message is unstoppable enthusiasm.
My message is ceaseless creation. I Am creation.
My message is wondrous amazement.
My message is unconditional kindness.
My message is instant forgiveness.

My message is hope for your suffering. Do not suffer. I Am not suffering.
My message is happiness for your tears. Do not cry. I Am not sadness.

I Am beauty. I Am joy.
I Am love. I Am favor.
I Am grace. I Am awe.

I reward unwavering faith.
I defeat all enemies.
I right all wrongs.

I deliver on My promises.

My promise is endless love.
My promise is indescribable joy.
My promise is awesome power.

My promise is unshakeable confidence.
My promise is abundant life.

Believe in Me. You will not lack.
Trust in Me. You will not lose.
Follow Me. You are guided.

Hold My hand. I Am always here with you.

I Am All There Is.

I Am God.

YOU ARE READY AND ABLE

Thank You for all You have given me.
Thank You for trusting me to carry out your mission.

I am honored. I am worthy. I am chosen.
I am glad. I am confident. I am ready. I am able.

You are ready and able:
To fight my battles.
To defeat my enemies.
To conquer darkness
To right all wrongs.

You are ready and able:
To deliver us your abundance.
To provide us your eternal hope.
To restore us with your loving grace.
To forgive us with your mercy and kindness.

You are ready and able:
To celebrate our victories.
To shower us with joy.
To sing with us, to dance with us.
To love with us, to create with us.

You are love. You are creation.
I am in You. You are in me.

Together we are One.

BE STILL AND BELIEVE

Be still and believe.
Be who you are.
Be like who made you. I made you.

Be kind. Be generous. Be loving.
Be caring. Be giving. Be hopeful.

Be miraculous. You are miraculous.

I created you for miracles.
I created you for greatness.
I created you for loving kindness.

I created you to experience My abundance.
I created you to experience My endless favor.

You are whole. You are complete.
You have everything you need to succeed.

You are ready for the journey. I Am on this journey with you.

Hold My hand. Together we will go far. Together we are unstoppable.

I Am the Great I Am and I Am inside of you.
You are inside of Me. I Am All There Is.

Together we are One.

EVERYTHING IS GOD

God is now. We are in God.
God is new. We are made new.
God is real. Our love is real.

God is aware. God is magic. God is miraculous.

God transforms. God heals.

God carries us. God lifts us. God holds us.

Our strength is in God.

God's strength is in our hands.

God is timeless. We are eternal.
God is peace. We are calm.
God is amazing. We are thankful.
God is abundance. We are loved.

God exceeds our dreams.
God orders our steps.
God clears our path.

God is everywhere. God is always here.

God Is All There Is. Everything Is God.

YOU ARE PERFECT IN MY EYES

I Am God calling out to you.

I Am here to inspire you.
I Am here to move you.
I Am here to love you.

Trust in Me. I trust in you.

I created you. I created all.

Everything is alive, everywhere you look.

The stars, the planets, the galaxies.
The trees, the oceans, the lands.
The sun, the moon, the clouds.
The birds, the fish, the animals.

Humanity is My greatest creation.

I gave you the power to feel Me.
I gave you the strength to reach Me.
I gave you the words to speak to Me.

I hear you. I see you.
I touch you. I hold you.
I power you. I move you.
I lift you. I carry you.

Hold My hand. I Am here for you.
Call out My name. I will move mountains for you.

I know no limits. I Am boundless.

I Am All There Is. I Am God.

▪▪▪

I created you in My image.

Your gifts are from Me. Your courage is from Me.

I Am joy. I Am courage.
I Am love. I love you.

You are perfect in My eyes. I made you.
You are My beauty. You are My magic.

I Am beauty. I Am magic.

Sing and dance. I Am your happiness.
Shout and praise. I Am your passion.
Love and serve. I Am your purpose.

I Am real. I Am All There Is. I Am God.

▪▪▪

When you see the stars in the sky, I Am here.
When you feel the warmth of the sun, I Am here.
When you feel the coolness of winds, I Am here.

When you prosper, I Am here. I feed you.
When you walk, I Am here. I power you.
When you love, I Am here. I Am in your heart.
When you forgive, I Am here. I Am your strength.
When you grieve, I Am here. I Am your comfort.

When you believe, I Am here. You see Me.

I see you. I hear you. I feel you. I love you.

I Am All There Is. I Am God.

▪▪▪

Beauty is everywhere. Love is everywhere. I Am everywhere.
Joy is everywhere. Prosperity is everywhere. I Am everywhere.

I Am everywhere you look. I Am in everyone.

I made everyone. I made all now, all there ever was, and all that will ever be.

I made you to feel Me.
I made you to share My love.
I made you to spread My message.

My message is opportunity.
My message is endless favor.
My message is boundless strength.
My message is ceaseless power.
My message is eternal peace.
My message is timeless answers.

I Am The Answer to questions not yet asked.

Speak with Me. I always hear you.
Open your heart. I always guide you.
Show your love. I always protect you.

My gifts are made real when you share the gifts I gave you.
My love is made real when your heart bursts with joy.
My courage is made real when you follow My path and hold My hand.

I Am your strength. I Am your courage.
I Am your joy. I Am your favor.

I Am the new. I Am the old. I Am forever.

I Am All There Is. I Am God.

▪▪▪

Know that I always love you.
Know that I always protect you.
Know that I Am always joyful for you.
Know that I sing with you so you may dance.

Know that I wake you so you may live your dreams.

■■■

I Am creation. I Am light. I Am energy.
I Am power. I Am strength. I Am courage.
I Am abundance. I Am favor. I Am opportunity.

I Am miraculous.

You are My miracle.

You have the capacity to walk with Me.
You have the understanding to know Me.

Speak My word. Say My name. I listen.

You cannot stumble when you walk with Me.
You cannot fail when you are thankful for Me.

You cannot move without Me. I power your steps.
You cannot believe without Me. I light your way.
You cannot dream without Me. I inspire your greatness.

I created you for greatness.

I created you with My strength and magic so you may know My power and experience My miracles.

I Am the joy in your heart.
I Am the energy that lifts you.
I Am the love that surrounds you.
I Am the abundance that favors you.
I Am the courage that forgives you.

I see you. I hear you. I touch you. I feel you.

Feel Me when you love. I Am your love.
Celebrate with Me when you are thankful. I Am your joy.

I lift you. I power you. I move you. I protect you.

Love Me when I shield you. I Am your protection.
Hold on to Me when I guide you. I Am the light on your path.

I Am your path. I Am The Way.
I Am your knowledge. I Am The Answer.
I Am your courage. I Am The Light.
I Am your truth. I Am peace.
I Am your joy. I Am happiness.
I Am your gratitude. I Am abundance.
I Am your strength. I Am power.
I Am your heart. I Am love.

I Am The Answer to questions not yet asked.
I Am the miracle for prayers not yet written.
I Am the magic for stars not yet born.
I Am the inspiration for dreams not yet real.
I Am the joy for celebrations not yet planned.
I Am the peace for struggles not yet experienced.
I Am the courage for cries not yet heard.
I Am the light for opportunity not yet seen.
I Am the energy for creations not yet made.

I Am creation. I Am life.

I Am All There Is.

I Am God.

DARE TO BE YOU

Celebrate Me. I celebrate you.
Embrace Me. I embrace you.
Love Me. I Am your heart.
Feel Me. I Am your hands.
Move with Me. I Am your breath.

▪▪▪

Have courage. I will light your path.
Have strength. I will power your steps.

Have trust. I will never leave you.
Have faith. I will never abandon you.

Have forgiveness. I will not judge you.
Have belief. I will not forsake you.

Have love. You are My love. I Am love.
Have joy. You are My joy. I Am joy.

Have peace. I Am your forgiveness.
Have confidence. I Am your answer.

▪▪▪

I made you on purpose. I Am not accident.
I made you to share My message.
I made you to spread My joy.

I made you to practice My love.

Forgive others. I forgive all.
Love others. I love all.

Trust in Me. I guide you. I guide all.

Experience Me. I Am All There Is.

I Am knowledge. I Am peace.
I Am song. I Am dance.
I Am light. I Am energy.
I Am truth. I Am courage.
I Am strength. I Am power.

I Am not lack. I Am abundance.

I do no evil. I Am pure joy.
I do no harm. I Am pure love.
I do not abandon. I Am pure trust.
I do not disappear. I Am pure faith.

■■■

Believe in Me. I believe in you. I made you.

See Me. I see you. Hear Me. I hear you.

Speak to Me. I listen. Cry to Me. I comfort.

Know Me. I know you.

I made you. I made all.

I made all there is, now, that ever was, and all that will ever be.

I Am the past. I Am the now. I Am the future.
I Am time. I Am space.
I Am wind. I Am rain.
I Am sky. I Am earth.
I Am clarity. I Am aware.
I Am peace. I Am love.
I Am moon. I Am sun.
I Am light. I Am energy.

I Am what is in your heart and on your path.
I Am your love. I Am your guide.

Follow Me and you will never be lost.
Dream with Me and you will never be discouraged.

Feel Me. I will touch you.
Open your heart. I will teach you.
Believe in My power. I will amaze you.
Cry out to Me. I will encourage you.
Release your pain. I will forgive you.

Walk My path. I will guide you.
Hold My hand. I will reward you.
Share My love. I will celebrate you.
Speak of My hope. I will deliver for you.

I never fail. I cannot fail.

I Am All There Is. I Am God.

▪▪▪

I need you so you may be greatness.
I forgive you so you may be clear.
I inspire you so you may dream.
I carry you so you may prosper.
I encourage you so you may wonder.
I embrace you so you may love.
I touch you so you may feel.

I hold you so you may release your gifts.
I power you so you may speak My truth.
I love you so you may share My love.

I provide for you so you may experience My endless favor.
I encourage you so you may understand My belief.

Believe in Me. I believe in you.

I created you. I created all.

I Am All There Is. I Am God.

■■■

I Am everywhere you look.
I Am every sound you hear.
I Am every word you speak.

I Am the air you breathe.
I Am the blood in your veins.
I Am the beating of your heart.

I Am the love for your enemies.
I Am the courage for your plans.
I Am the wonder for your dreams.

I lift you. I Am the sky.
I move you. I Am the earth.
I hold you. I Am the oceans.
I amaze you. I Am the moon. I Am the stars.
I light you. I Am the sun.

I embolden you. I Am your confidence.
I embrace you. I Am your love.
I answer you. I Am your truth.

I know you. Know Me and I will not leave you.

Believe in Me. I will fulfill the promise I've given you.
Share your gifts. I will provide you endless favor.
Spread your wings. I will provide the air so you may fly.
Hold on to your faith. I will provide the strength for you to thrive.

Live your dreams. I Am endless opportunity.

I Am All There Is. I Am God.

■■■

Love one another. I Am in everyone.
Encourage one another. I lift everyone.
Dance with one another. I celebrate everyone.
Forgive one another. I forgive everyone.
Comfort one another. I relieve everyone.

Spread joy. I Am gladness.
Share love. I Am hope.
Dream big. I Am courage.

Believe in Me. I Am real.
Hear Me when I speak. I listen.
Move when I inspire. I Am strength.

Create and I will amaze.
Forgive and I will hold you.

▪▪▪

Dare to dream. Dare to dance. Dare to believe.

Dare to celebrate. Dare to be alive. I Am alive.
Dare to wonder. Dare to explore. I Am confidence.
Dare to question. Dare to know. I Am trust.
Dare to move. Dare to fly. I Am opportunity.
Dare to walk. Dare to run. I Am energy.
Dare to see. Dare to taste. I Am beauty.
Dare to feel. Dare to love. I Am light.
Dare to prosper. Dare to give thanks. I Am abundance.

Dare to be you. I Am in you. I made you.

Walk with Me. I Am your guide.
Love with Me. I Am your heart.
Move with Me. I Am your power.

Trust in Me. I will reward your faith.
Believe in Me. I will light your way.

I Am All There Is. I Am God.

I Am in you. You are in Me.

Together we are One.

YOU ARE REAL

Thank you God for ordering my steps.
Thank you God for lighting my way.
Thank you God for rewarding my belief.
Thank you God for forgiving my sins.
Thank you God for providing my faith.
Thank you God for answering my call.

You are the answer for questions not yet asked.
You are the truth for discoveries not yet made.
You are the life for babies not yet born.

You are the light for souls returning to You.

You heal. You comfort. You amaze.

You inspire my dreams. You share your gifts.

You are love. You are joy.
You are my love. You are my joy.

You are strength. You are knowledge.
You are my strength. You are my knowledge.

I am in You.

You are in me.

Together we are One.

■■■

You are real. I believe.
You are here. I know.
You are everywhere. I see.
You are love. I feel.
You are joy. I celebrate.
You are music. I dance.
You are land. I explore.

You comfort when I cry.
You forgive when I sin.
You amaze when I believe.
You transform when I wonder.
You encourage when I doubt.
You strengthen when I am weak.

You love when I open my heart and share your love.
You speak when I open my mouth and share your message.
You provide when I open my gifts and share your favor.

I am thankful:

To know You. To trust You.
For You know me. You feel me.

To love You. To celebrate You.
For You love me. You celebrate me.

To trust in You. To believe in You.

For You made me. You have faith in me. I have faith in You.
For You move me. You have strength in me. I have strength in You.
For You energize me. You breathe life in me. I have life in You.
For You encourage me. You put dreams in me. I wake with You.

I am in You. You are in me.

You are God. I am grateful.

Together we are One.

I MATTER FOR YOU

I am pure consciousness.

I am a channel for your good.
I am a channel for your love.
I am a channel for your grace.

I am a messenger of your unlimited power.

Of your unlimited opportunity.
Of your endless promises.
Of your eternal favor.
Of your timeless answers.

I ask and I receive.

I stand and You deliver.

You stand with me and I deliver for You.

God, you love me. You care for me.
You matter to me. I matter for You.

You create my todays.
You brighten my tomorrows.
You forgive my yesterdays.
You hold my future in your hand.
You wash away my sins with your unconditional love.

I am in You. You are in me.

Together we are One.

▪▪▪

My success is my destiny.
My destiny is to empower.
My destiny is to enlighten.
My destiny is to uplift.
My destiny, my success, is guaranteed.

Connection is assured.
Connection is complete.

I am complete. I am equipped with all that I need.

All of my needs are met always.

I am with You.
You are with me.

Together we are One.

YOU ARE A GIFT

You are a gift.
You are important.
You matter.

I created you to matter.
I created you to inspire so you may inspire others.
I created you to challenge so you may challenge others to live the greatness that is their destiny.

Everyone is complete as I created everyone. I created all. I created you.

You are a miracle. You are incredible.

Humanity is My greatest creation.

I created you to love.
I created you to feel.
I created you to share.
I created you to experience My abundance.
I created you to experience My endless favor.

Count on your tomorrow, as I make your dreams real today.

I Am real. My love for you is real.
I Am All There Is. I Am God.

You are in Me. I Am in you.
Together we are One.

OUR DESTINY BEGINS NOW

If God is infinite, then so can be my dreams.

If God creates all, then so does He create my plans.
If God fulfills all, then so does He fulfill my wishes.
If God sustains all, then so does He sustain my faith.
If God is true, then so does He inspire my confidence.

If God answers all prayer, then my belief is not in vain.
If God heals all hearts, then my love is pure.
If God provides all, then my abundance is assured.
If God forgives all, then my mistakes are wiped away.
If God remembers all, then I am never forgotten.
If God commands all, then my strength is boundless.
If God directs all, then my trust is well-placed.

If God Is All There Is, then I am destined for greatness.

God is great. All is well. Love is pure.

Energy is abundant. Creation is eternal.
Time is boundless. Success is assured.

▪▪▪

Our destiny begins now.

Truth is here. Hope is now. Life is joy.
Light is endless. Beauty is everywhere.

Our destiny is made real.

Confidence is within. Once the prayer is made, the promise is done.

Belief is rewarded. Victory is celebrated.

We are held in love. We are One in God.
We are pure of heart. We are clear of vision.

Our future is now.

Our courage is bottomless.
Our possibility is limitless.
Our destiny is timeless.

God is with us and within us. Everything is God.

We touch God when we feel.

God holds us when we move.
God directs us when we create.

God is moved when we love.
God is boundless.
God is sky. God is earth.

Our destiny is in God.

■■■

God moves mountains.
God calms seas.

God relieves our pain.
God clears our path.
God delivers our miracles.
God celebrates our joy.
God orders our steps.
God hears our prayers.

Our answer is God.

We are all in God.

God is in all of us.

Everything is God.

Our destiny is true. God is true.
Our destiny is love. God is love.
Our destiny is here. God is here.

God is with us. God is within us.

God Is All There Is.

We are One in God.

I AM HOLDING YOU IN LOVE

I Am holding you in love.
I Am holding you in confidence.

You are My child. You are a gift.

I've given you gifts to share.
I'm showing you roads to explore.
I'm making openings where there were none.

Your path is made clear by Me.
Your worries are washed away by Me.
Your destiny is ordered by Me.

Everything you need I Am giving you.

I provide. I heal. I bless. I transform.

I make old new. I birth new opportunity.

I turn darkness into light.
I destroy your enemies.
I cure your sickness.

I marvel at you when you marvel at Me.

Abundance is yours when you give thanks to Me.

Love overflows for you when you open your heart for Me.

Opportunity knows no bounds just as My sky knows no limits.

I Am time. I Am space.
I Am wind. I Am rain.
I Am sun. I Am earth.

I Am the moon and the glow.
I Am the oceans and the tides.
I Am the leaves and the trees.
I Am the night and the day.

I Am All and In All.

I Am All There Is.

▪▪▪

I Am in you.

Everything I Am, you are.

You have everything that I Am.

I give you all. I see all. I hear all.

I wipe your tears.
I comfort your cries.
I heal your pain.
I celebrate your gladness.
I love your joy.
I champion your talent.
I right your wrongs.
I clear your hurdles.
I calm your anxiety.

I lift you up when you fall.
I catch you when you rise.

I power your steps.
I order your chaos.

I love you, when you love Me and do not love Me.
I protect you, when you believe in Me, and when you disbelieve.

Your journey is My journey. I Am with you.

I Am always with you. I Am in you.
You are in Me.
Together we are One.

■■■

I rise with you. I stand with you.
I leap with you. I fly with you. I soar with you.

Soar in My skies filled with love.
Swim in My oceans filled with peace.

Dance to My music made with joy.
Walk on My earth created with wonder.

■■■

Listen to your heart. I hear it beating. Your heart is My heart.

Feel the blood in your veins.

I move you. I power you. Your blood is My blood.

Drink My living water and eat from My bread. I feed you. I sustain you.

Do not worry. Do not fear. I am not worry. I am not fear.

Love and you will be loved. I Am love.
Sing and you will be heard. I Am alive.
Shout and call out My name. I Am here.

I Am everywhere.
I Am All There Is.
I Am God.

Everything I Am, you are.

I Am inside of you.
You are inside of Me.
Together we are One.

YOU ARE CREATED TO BE FREE

I create heavens and stars. I Am creation.

I Am wonder and awe.
I Am celebration and joy.
I Am love and hope.
I Am ecstasy and abundance.
I Am radiance and beauty.

I shine when you shine. I adore you.
I make miracles when you believe. I astonish you.
I make music so you may dance. I bless you.
I calm your mind so you may listen. I heal you.

I power your steps so you can move. I Am courage.
I forgive your sins. I Am grace.
I heal your heart. I Am your cure.
I provide your abundance. I Am favor. I Am mercy and kindness.

I Am open. I Am available. I Am here with you.

Open your heart and let Me in.

Cry out My name and I will provide.
Love Me and I will love you.
Sing and I will dance with you.
Worry and I will calm you.
Believe and I will amaze you.
Trust in Me and I will astonish you.

■■■

I hold you in My hand. I hold you in love.

You are whole. You are worthy.

Everything I Am is inside of you.

I made you on purpose, in My likeness and image, so you can bring Me joy, and to the world, peace and love and hope.

I give you opportunity so you can share My love.
I open your heart so you can shine as My stars.

I fill you with dreams so you can inspire greatness in others and be greatness.

I kiss you and cover you with My favor so you can marvel at My beauty and be beauty.

I forgive your sins and shower you with My mercy so you may be merciful.

Show the world your gifts. They are yours to share.
Demonstrate your belief and I will demonstrate My magic.
Believe in My miracles and I will astonish your capacity to believe.

■■■

Nothing is impossible for Me.

No dream is too big or small for Me.
No prayer goes unheard by Me.
No tear goes unseen by Me.
No cry goes uncomforted by Me.
No sin goes unforgiven by Me.

You are loved. I love you. I Am love.
You are celebrated. I celebrate you. I Am joy.
You are provided for. I provide for you. I Am abundance.
You are a miracle. I created you. I Am creation.

I birthed you with My eye so I could see you do great things.
My greatness is in you.

I comfort you with My love so you can share your gifts, and My love.

I Am your courage.

Fear not. Want not. I always provide.
Cry not. Worry not. I always comfort.

Believe in hope. Believe in peace. I Am hope. I Am peace.
Surrender in love. Surrender in joy. I Am love. I Am joy.

Cry out in thanksgiving. I Am gratitude.

Walk My path. I Am the light of the stars.
Swim My ocean. I Am the water. I Am the tide.

My water is living water.
My bread is sustenance.
My favor is pure.
My possibility is limitless.

You are courageous. I walk with you.
You are fearless. I run with you.
You are powerful. I move mountains for you.
You are greatness. I astonish with miracles for you.

You are My pride. You are My joy.
You are My child. You are My love.

All children are My children.
All creation is My creation. I create all. I Am creation.
All celebration is My celebration. I celebrate all. I Am joy.

I astonish. I amaze. I thrill when you seek Me.

■■■

Have no fear, for I Am always here with you.

I Am forever inside you, as you are an eternal being created in My likeness and image.

You are created to be free.

You are here to soar, to shine, to explore, to grow, to give, to experience all of My wonders and lands.

Dare to explore. I will inspire you.
Dare to dream. I will wake you.

Dare to be bold. I Am your passion. I Am your courage.

I Am your heat when you are cold.
I Am your heart when you love.
I Am your mercy when you forgive.
I Am your miracle when you believe.
I Am your peace when you trust.
I Am your calm when you fear.

Do not fear. I am not fear.
Do not sin. I am not sin.

I Am wonder. I Am power.
I Am awe. I Am beauty.
I Am joy. I Am abundance.

I Am endless favors and eternal tomorrows.
I Am the peace and opportunity inside your todays.
I Am the forgiveness that rights the wrongs in your yesterdays.

I Am the past. I Am the present. I Am the future.
I Am the here. I Am the now.
I Am the near. I Am the far.

I Am All There Is, all there ever was, and all will ever be.

■■■

I smile for you. You are My happiness.
I sing for you. You are My music.
I laugh for you. You are My joy.
I shine for you. You are My light.
I love for you. You are My heart.
I create for you. You are My life.
I forgive for you. You are My mercy.
I open doors for you. You are My kindness.
I move mountains for you. You are My power.

You are here for a reason.

I created you for a purpose.
I made you for greatness, with My greatness.
I believe in you so you may encourage others to believe in Me.

Celebrate My miracles and I will provide endless miracles.
Share My love and I will clothe you in My radiant love.
Proclaim My favor and I will give you endless favor and opportunity.

My bounty is your bounty.

You shall never be hungry when you sit at My table.
You shall never be thirsty when you drink My wine and My living water.

My bread is your bread. My joy is your joy.

My hand is your hand. Your hand is in mine.

Together we will go far.
Together we are unstoppable.
Together we are One.

EXPECT AND YOU WILL RECEIVE

I Am God.

I Am in you and you are in Me.

I Am in all. I Am All There Is. I Am the Great I Am.

Believe and you will see. Trust and I will amaze.

Pray and you will be provided for.
Give thanks and My gratitude will provide your abundance.

Expect and you will receive. It is given as soon as the prayer is made.

Count on Me.

I hear you. I see you. I touch you. I feel you. I love you.

I Am All There Is. I Am God.

You are in Me. I Am in you. Together we are One.

■■■

Where boldness reigns, I reign.
Where mercy reigns, I reign.
Where love reigns, I reign.
Where kindness reigns, I reign.
Where hope reigns, I reign.

I restore wholeness with My mercy and kindness.
I make miracles with your faith and belief.

I astonish with My power. I energize with My light.

I carry you when you fall. I Am your strength when you have none.
I celebrate you when you dance. I Am your joy when you have plenty.
I love you when you open. I Am your heart when you share of My love.

When your heart expands, My love expands.
When your trust expands, My possibility expands.

Open your eyes and see Me everywhere.
Open your ears and hear Me in all.
Open your hand and feel My touch.
Open your mind and know My presence.
Open your heart and share My love.

Be open. Be available.

I Am always available.
I Am always ready. I Am always able.

I Am God.

You are in Me and I Am in you.
Together we are One.

I SURRENDER TO YOUR JOY

Thank You God, for all You have given me.

Thank You God, for all my prayers You have heard and answered.
Thank You God, for all my sins You have washed clean with your mercy and grace.

Your favor is pure.
Your love is real.

I surrender to your joy, and You provide me with more joy.
I celebrate your wonder and awe, and You shine your sun and stars.

I believe and I see You.
I touch and I feel You.
I listen and I hear You.

When I stumble, You catch me. You right my steps.

When I am lost, You direct me. You Are The Way. You order my path.
When I am confused, You answer me. You Are The Answer. You are truth.
When I am overwhelmed, You calm me. You Are The Light. You are peace.

You are the light in all. You conquer all darkness.
You are the happiness in all. You comfort all sadness.
You are the forgiveness in all. You strengthen all weakness.

Thank You for inspiring me. I aspire to your greatness.
Thank You for believing in me. I trust in your plan.

You are my guide.
Lead me on your path.
My journey is your journey.
I know my destiny is in You.

Thank You God, for I am in You, and You are in me.

Together we are One.

I CREATED YOU FOR GREATNESS

My breath is your breath.
My blood is your blood.
My courage is your courage.
My hope is your hope.
My faith is your faith.

I answer your questions. I Am The Answer.
I open your doors. I Am The Way.
I brighten your path. I Am The Light.
I astonish your belief. I Am The Truth.

■■■

I Am creation.

You are My creation.

I created you with purpose and vision.
I created you for greatness.

Share My wonder, and I will show you awe.
Share My love, and I will show you power.
Share My mercy, and I will show you kindness.
Share My comfort, and I will show you courage.
Share My hope, and I will show you opportunity.
Share My abundance, and I will show you treasure.
Share My joy, and I will show you unbridled bliss.

Nothing is impossible for Me.

I Am all possibility. I Am all creation.

I Am All. I Am.

Everything I Am is inside of you.

I created you in My likeness and image.

I Am in everyone.

I Am always here even when you do not see Me or hear Me.
I Am always with you even when you do not feel Me or touch Me.

I Am real, even when you do not sense Me.

I make miracles, even when you do not believe.
I move mountains, even when you do not trust.
I open hearts, even when you do not love.
I heal wounds, even when you have given up.

I forgive sins, even when you do not.

My forgiveness is My grace and kindness.

My love is your love. I Am love.
My joy is your joy. I Am joy.
My hope is your hope. I Am hope.
My abundance is your abundance. I Am abundance.

My energy is your energy. I Am light.
My truth is your truth. I Am The Answer.
My clarity is your clarity. I Am The Way.
My birth is your birth. I Am creation.

■■■

My power is in you. I Am in you. I Am power.
My courage is in you. I Am in you. I Am courage.
My peace is in you. I Am in you. I Am peace.
My love is in you. I Am in you. I Am love.
My beauty is in you. I Am in you. I Am beauty.

You are beautiful to Me. I made you in My likeness and image.

I have faith in you. I created you on purpose.

Have faith in Me. Let Me guide you.

Let Me power you. Let Me embolden you.
Let Me amaze you. Let Me astonish you.
Let Me love you. Let Me open you.

I Am preparing you. I Am leading you.

Your path is My path. I Am The Way.

I Am The Answer to your questions not yet asked.

I will make a way where you see no way.
I will open hearts when they are closed.
I will encourage when you are met with disbelief.

■■■

Do not worry.
Do not fear.
Do not lie still.

I walk with you.
I run with you.
I dance with you.
I leap with you.
I fly with you.

Soar in My skies filled with My love.

My air is your air. I Am the air.
My light is your light. I Am the light.

Trust in My power. Trust in My plan. Trust in Me.
Believe in My message. Believe in My promise. Believe in Me.

Receive My guidance and wisdom, and I will give you eternal favor.
Share My hope and possibility, and I will reward your belief.
Dance to My music and I will provide you endless joy and celebration.

Your courage comes from Me. I Am courage.
Your faith comes from Me. I Am faith.
Your kindness comes from Me. I Am kindness.
Your eternity comes from Me. I Am eternity.
Your favor comes from Me. I Am favor.
Your energy comes from Me. I Am energy.

I Am The Light.
I Am The Way.
I Am The Truth.

I Am All There Is.

You are in Me. I Am in you.
Together we are One.

I EXPAND MY FAITH

I no longer doubt. I believe with my whole heart.
I outstretch my hands. I expand my faith.

You are real. You are true.
You are my Father. I am your child.

You guide me. You protect me. You love me.

You trust me with your mission. Thank You God.
You embolden me with your courage. Thank You God.
You enlighten me with your wisdom. Thank You God.
You inspire me with your message. Thank You God.

Your message is hope in times of hate.
Your message is peace in times of war.
Your message is strength in times of weakness.
Your message is faith in times of darkness.

I receive your message so I may share it.

Thank You, for all You have given me to share, and continue to give me, now and forever.

I am your servant. You are my master.

Thank You God for your direction.
Thank You God for your protection.
Thank You God for your bounty.

My enthusiasm for You is boundless.
My belief in You is endless.
My love for You is timeless.

For this I am thankful, as I am in You, and You are in me.

Together we are One.

ALL IS WELL, ALL IS GOOD

The greatness of God is expressing itself as my life.

The fullness of God is expressing itself in the richness of my experiences.

The wholeness of God is expressing itself in the depths of my loving relationships.

The grace of God is expressing itself in His unconditional forgiveness.

The courage of God is expressing itself in my strength overcoming obstacles.

The abundance of God is expressing itself in the countless opportunities I encounter.

The love of God is expressing itself in the hearts of everyone on my path who walk in truth.

The hope of God is expressing itself in my boundless joy and enthusiasm.

The will of God operates through my life today.
The hand of God touches me in my life today.
The mind of God leads me in my life today.
The heart of God opens me in my life today.
The joy of God encourages me in my life today.

God is in me. God is All There Is.

God is in everyone.
God is all there ever was or will be.

God is everywhere.
God is creation.
God created all.
God created us for greatness.
God leads us for greatness.
God inspires us to do great things.

God's work is our work.
God works through all.
God is everywhere.

We are in God. All is God.

God Is All There Is.

All is well. All is good.

Together we are One.

WALK IN CONFIDENCE

I Am God calling out to you.

Celebrate My miracles and I will show you more miracles.
Discover My wonders and I will show you more wonders.

Dance to My music and I will give you courage to sing My song.

I will lift your voice. I will order your steps. I will compose your masterpiece.

You are My masterpiece.

I created you to accomplish greatness.

Do My work and you will see.
Open your heart and you will feel.
Lift your eyes and you will believe.

■■■

Walk in confidence. I Am your confidence. I Am confidence.
Love without limits. I Am your courage. I Am courage.

Stumble and I will catch you.

When you feel lost, know that I've never lost you.

I cannot, I will not ever lose you.

Follow Me and you will dream.
Hear Me and you will know.
Touch Me and you will feel.

Lose your way and I will direct you.
Lose your courage and I will inspire you.
Lose your footing and I will lift you.
Lose your belief and and I will encourage you.

Encounter Me everywhere. See Me in everyone.

I see you. I always see you. I always see everyone.

I Am everywhere you look.
I Am everywhere you walk.
I Am everywhere you work.

When you work, know I Am at work.
When you love, know I Am at the center of your heart.
When you believe, know I Am speaking to you in truth.

I Am true. I Am always true.
I Am always here. I never disappear.
I Am All There Is and all there will ever be.

I Am God.
You are in Me. I Am in you.
Together we are One.

■■■

Open your heart and feel Me.
Open your hand and touch Me.
Open your eyes and see Me.
Open your ears and hear Me.

Open your mouth and speak My truth.

I will give you the words to say when you have no words.

I promise you wholeness. I Am wholeness.

You are whole. You are worthy of Me.

I made you in My likeness and image.

Your greatness is in Me. My greatness is in you.

I Am always present. I Am All There Is.

▪▪▪

Know that I Am always here with you.
Feel that I Am always inside your heart.
Believe that I Am always doing great things in your life.

My promise is real. I Am your promise.
My love is real. I Am your love.
My joy is real. I Am your joy.
My abundance is real. I Am your abundance.
My strength is real. I Am your strength.

My possibilities are real. I Am possibility. I Am endless.

My miracles are real. I can do anything as I create everything.

Nothing is impossible for Me. Greatness is unstoppable for Me.

My miracles are your happiness.

You are a miracle.

Be happy. Be loving. Be open.
Be available. Be courageous.
Be hopeful. Be caring. Be forgiving.
Be kind. Be joyful. Be bold.

I Am boundless. I Am in you.

Together we are One.

▪▪▪

Celebrate My work and I will inspire your great work.

Your work is My work. I created you for a purpose.

I Am leading you toward your greatness and your purpose.

You are already great. You are made in My image.

I made you with My hands.
I strengthen you with My courage.
I power you with My love.
I open you with My touch.
I encourage you with My truth.
I lead you with My magic.
I celebrate you with My joy.

I provide for you with your belief.

Believe in Me. I believe in you.
Know Me. I know you.

I Am inside of you.
I Am inside of everyone.

You are inside of Me.

Everyone and everything now and always is inside of Me.

I Am everything.
I Am All There Is.
I Am God.

Together we are One.

■■■

Fall and I will catch you.
Leap and I will fly with you.
Jump and I will amaze you.

Believe and I will never leave you.
Forgive and I will never abandon you.
Walk and I will never misdirect you.
Question and I will never mislead you.

I Am The Answer for questions not yet asked.

I Am the truth inside problems not yet solved.
I Am the love inside hearts not yet open.

I Am the purity inside babies not yet born.
I Am the miracles inside prayers not yet made.
I Am the possibility inside wishes not yet fulfilled.
I Am the joy inside dreams not yet lived.
I Am the beauty inside art not yet completed.

I Am The Way. I Am The Light.
I Am The Answer. I Am The Truth.
I Am creation. I Am in all.
I Am All There Is.
I Am God.

I Am in you. You are in Me.

Together we are One.

I AM ALWAYS INSIDE YOU

See with My eyes. You will never be lost.
Love with My heart. You will never be closed.

Dream with My imagination and My possibility will always be yours.

I Am possibility. I Am kindness.

Forgive with My love and I will never leave you. I cannot, I will not ever leave you.

I always love you. I Am love.
I always lead you. I Am The Way.
I always encourage you. I Am The Truth.
I always provide for you. I Am The Answer.
I always deliver for you. I Am abundance.

I always walk with you. I Am your feet.
I always stand with you. I Am your courage.
I always rise with you. I Am your trust.
I always perform miracles for you. I Am your belief.
I always inspire you. I Am your hope.
I always celebrate you. I Am your joy.
I always energize you. I Am your power.

I power you. I Am light.
I lead you. I Am truth.
I encourage you. I Am The Answer.
I promise you. I Am The Way.

My way is your way.

Follow Me and never be lost.
Swim in My oceans and you will never drown.
Soar in My skies and you will never fall.

Love with My heart and you will feel My love everywhere and in everyone.
Give with My hands and you will receive My abundance everywhere you go.
See with My eyes and you will see greatness in everyone.
Walk with My feet and you will be inspired everywhere you go.

Discover My path. I Am everywhere you go.
Celebrate My miracles. I Am everywhere you look.
Dance to My music. I Am the joy in everything.
Forgive with My strength. I Am the love in every heart.
Pray with My trust. I Am the belief behind every dream.
Open with My possibility. I Am the opportunity behind every door.

Knock and I will let you in.

▪▪▪

I Am already inside you. I Am always inside you.

Know that always, and you will know Me always.
Feel that always, and you will feel Me always.
Believe that always, and I will always deliver My miracles.

Create with Me always and I will always inspire your art.

Dream with Me always and I will always awaken your purpose and greatness.

Love with Me always and your heart will always expand with My endless love and promise.

Walk with Me always and your courage will always strengthen with My strength and truth.

My truth is eternal. I Am eternal.
My possibility is endless. I Am endless.
My joy is boundless. I Am boundless.
My power is limitless. I Am limitless.

My heart is open when you open your heart.
My path is clear when you walk with confidence.
My direction is true when you believe with conviction.

My miracles are made when you trust.
My celebrations are planned when you dance.
My beauty is seen when you create.
My love is felt when you touch.
My way is experienced when you forgive.

I Am The Way. I Am forgiveness.

I Am your courage when you have no courage.
I Am your joy when you have no joy.
I Am your power when you have no energy.
I Am your light when you cannot see.
I Am your knowledge when you cannot hear.
I Am your abundance when you do not taste.
I Am your food when you are hungry.
I Am your tears when you release your pain.

▪▪▪

I comfort you. I Am comfort.
I strengthen you. I Am strength.
I energize you. I Am energy.
I move you. I Am movement.

I made you. I Am All There Is.

I made all. I Am all, now, all there ever was, and all there will ever be.

I Am the future. I Am the past.
I Am the rain. I Am the sun.
I Am the moon. I Am the stars.

I Am everywhere you look.

I Am every time you feel.
I Am every miracle you celebrate.

I Am every possibility for that you are grateful.

Be thankful and I deliver My gifts for you.

Open your gifts and feel My love.
Give of yourself and you will know My generosity.
Create your art and you will understand My beauty.
Live your dreams and you will experience My wonder.
Believe with your all and you will live in My kingdom.

■■■

My kingdom is yours. Everything is yours.

Knock and you will enter.

Open My door and never close.
Open your heart and always love.

I love you. I Am your love. I Am love.
I celebrate you. I Am your dance. I Am your music.
I Am celebration. I Am joy.

Believe in My possibility.

I Am your possibility. I Am all possibility.

I Am endless imagination.
I Am ceaseless wonder.
I Am miraculous awe.

You are My vessel. You are My joy.
You are My heart. You are My love.
You are My possibility. You are My creation.

My greatness is in you.

MY ANSWER IS ALWAYS TRUE

Your destiny is set before you dream.
Your path is clear before you wake.
Your choice is true before you walk.
Your steps are ordered before you run.

My sky is yours. Leap and you will fly.
My air is yours. Jump and you will soar.
My trust is yours. Believe and I will deliver.
My truth is yours. Know and you will never be lost.

■■■

See Me everywhere. Feel Me everywhere.

See Me in the sun. Feel Me in the wind.
See Me in the stars. Feel Me in the oceans.
See Me in the rainbows. Feel Me in the midst of your storms
and I will deliver you.

My promise never expires.
My possibility never ends.
My creation never ceases.
My beauty never fades.
My belief never wavers.
My heart never hardens.
My hands never close.
My trust never doubts.

Believe. I always deliver.
Give. I always provide.
Touch. I always feel.
Open. I always love.

▪▪▪

Stay in truth. Stay strong.
I Am truth. I Am strength.

Walk in courage. Live with fullness.
I Am courage. I Am complete.

My love is complete when you love with My heart.
My universe expands when you create with My beauty.
My possibility is endless when you dream with My imagination.

Celebrate Me. I celebrate you.
Believe in Me. I believe in you.

I created you for purpose and for greatness.

My intent is always pure.
My answer is always true.

I Am The Answer. I Am truth.

My love is always strong.
My courage is always available.
My possibility is always attainable.

Everything I created you for, I know you can do.

I made you in My likeness and image.

Know that I Am always with you. I Am always inside of you.

You are always in Me. I cannot, I will not ever leave you.
You are always led. I never misdirect you.
You are always forgiven. I never lose faith in you.
You are always worthy. I never think less of you.

You are always strong.

I power your drive.
I order your steps.
I clear your path.
I open your mind.
I unlock your heart.
I deliver your abundance.
I celebrate your joy.
I beautify your world.
I create your art.
I imagine your dreams.
I encourage your faith.
I answer your questions.

▪▪▪

I Am The Answer for questions not yet asked.

I answer your prayers for prayers not yet made.
I heal your wounds for hurts not yet felt.
I encourage your belief for miracles not yet seen.

I open your heart for experiences not yet real.
I open your mind for truth not yet known.
I open your eyes to see My light in darkness.

I free your burdens for strength not yet needed.
I forgive your sins for errors not yet made.
I provide your bounty for feasts not yet planned.
I celebrate your joy for dreams not yet lived.
I wipe your tears for cries not yet wailed.
I clear your path for feet not yet stumbled.

I show My possibility through doors not yet opened.
I deliver My favor through belief not yet complete.
I unlock My treasure through abundance not yet celebrated.

I promise My miracles for your prayers.
I open My heart for your love.
I deliver My wonder for your trust.
I provide My guidance for your sight.

I shine My light so you have faith.
I demonstrate My miracles so you have belief.
I share My truth so you have knowledge.

SEEK AND FIND ME

Seek and find Me.

I Am not hidden. I Am real.
I Am everywhere you look.

I Am the love you experience.
I Am the power that moves you when you walk.
I Am the light that energizes you when you believe.
I Am the wonder that amazes you when you wake from your dreams.
I Am the clarity that surrounds you when you explore My lands.
I Am the beauty you see when you admire My creation.
I Am the boldness that envelops you when you need strength.
I Am the faith that encourages you when you hope with all of your heart.
I Am the joy that celebrates you when you dance to My music.

I Am in the miracles you see every day.
I Am on the paths you walk in every direction.

All paths lead to Me.
All doors open to Me.
All skies expand to Me.
All stars light to Me.

All power comes from Me. I Am energy.
All creation comes from Me. I Am beauty.
All wisdom comes from Me. I Am truth.
All abundance comes from Me. I Am the bounty for your harvest.

Feast at My table and never go hungry.
Drink My Living Water so you shall live in My fullness.

▪▪▪

I Am here for you. I Am always here.
I Am here for everyone. I Am inside of everyone.

I made you. I made everyone.
I made all. I Am All.

I made greatness so you may be great.
I made purpose so you may live your purpose.
I made courage so you may be strong.
I made music so you may dance.
I made joy so you may celebrate.

I made belief so you may know Me.
I made love so you may feel Me.
I made words so you may reach Me.

▪▪▪

I hold you in My hand.
I whisper in your ear.

I comfort when you cry.
I amaze when you believe.
I astonish when you trust.

I right all wrongs when you sin.
I forgive all mistakes when you are misled.

Know that I Am truth.

Follow Me and be led.
Hear Me and be guided.
Trust Me and be inspired.
Believe Me and be powerful.

Sit at My table and be fed.
Share in My truth and be wise.
Pray in My name and be heard.
Walk on My lands and be moved.

Soar in My skies and be held by My air.

My wind will direct you.
My sun will light you.
My stars will inspire you.
My love will open you.

My wonders will capture your amazement.
My miracles will earn your trust.
My forgiveness will wipe away your sins.

My hands are open to hold you.
My possibility is endless to awaken you.
My courage is bountiful to embolden you.
My answers are clear to guide you.
My miracles are here to astonish you.

▪▪▪

I Am here to lift you.

I Am magic when you believe.
I Am faith when you trust.
I Am happiness when you laugh.
I Am music when you dance.

I Am the power when you are lifted by My wings.

You are made to fly.
You are ready to soar.
You are worthy to matter.

You are wise to lead others. I lead you.
You are open to love others. I love you.
You are kind to forgive others. I forgive you.
You are bold to inspire others. I inspire you.
You are powerful to strengthen others. I strengthen you.

You are worthy to live the promise of greatness that I give you.
You are whole to receive the promise of abundance that I reward you.

Your mind is clear so you may know My wisdom.
You heart is open so you may feel My love.
Your destiny is real so you may live My purpose.

■■■

Trust in Me so I may complete My works.
Believe in Me so I may demonstrate My wonders.

Follow Me. I will direct your steps.

Speak My truth. I will strengthen your voice.
I will give you words to say when you have no words.

Live in My world. My world is your world.
Swim in My oceans. My Living Water is pure for you.
Shine in My light. My energy is power for you.

■■■

Believe in My possibility. I Am all possibility.

I can do anything because I made everything.

I Am in all because I Am All There Is.
I see all because I Am everywhere.
I feel all because I Am in everyone.
I forgive all because I open everyone.
I direct all because I know what you are capable of.

You are capable for greatness as My greatness is in you.
You are made for purpose as My purpose is what made you.
You are here to lead as My knowledge is what leads you.

■■■

Dare to dream. My imagination inspires you.
Dare to explore. My courage directs you.
Dare to love. My heart opens you.
Dare to forgive. My mercy cleanses you.
Dare to ask. My answers embolden you.
Dare to create. My abundance rewards you.

Dare to soar. My air lifts you. I Am the air.
Dare to shine. My light energizes you. I Am the light.
Dare to move. My path is clear for you. I Am The Way.
Dare to lead. My wisdom is real for you. I Am the truth.

Dare to live. My eternity is waiting for you. I Am eternal.

Dare to be great. I made you for greatness.
Dare to love fully. I provide you for purpose.

I love you. I Am love. Your love is in Me.

I Am in you. I Am in all.
I Am in everyone.

I Am All There Is.

You are in Me.

I Am All.
I Am God.

I AM GRATEFUL FOR ALL THAT YOU GIVE

I am thankful. Thank You for your words.
I am led. Thank You for your guidance.
I am fed. Thank You for your bountiful wisdom.
I am amazed. Thank You for your possibilities.
I am encouraged. Thank You for your faith in me.
I am needed. Thank You for your purpose in me.
I am faithful. Thank You for your trust in me.
I am able. Thank You for your energy in me.

Thank You God for creating me.
Thank You God for loving me.
Thank You God for opening me.
Thank You God for directing me.
Thank You God for encouraging me.

Thank You God, for your possibility shows up as my life.
Thank You God, for your truth is clear in my mind.
Thank You God, for your power is lighting my way.

You are The Way.
You are All There Is.

I am in You.
You are in me.

For this and more, I am thankful.

Together we are One.

▪▪▪

Your words lift me.
Your truth answers me.
Your possibility amazes me.
Your miracles astonish me.
Your inspiration emboldens me.
Your beauty lightens me.
Your forgiveness reshapes me.
Your knowledge renews me.
Your trust leads me.
Your love opens me.

My heart is your heart.

I know You are in my heart and I am in your heart.

Your wisdom guides me.
Your creation envelops me.
Your joy celebrates me.

When I speak, I know You listen.
When I hear, I know You lead.
When I know, I know You provide.
When I cry, I know You comfort.
When I believe, I know You deliver.
When I stumble, I know You forgive.

For this and more, I am grateful.
I am grateful for all that You give.

I am in You. You are in me.
You are in all. You are All There Is.
Together we are One.

I AM RECEIVING MY YES

An affirmation gifted through me from Spirit:

I have a strong energetic inner knowing that there is something magical and transformative birthing itself in my life right now.

I know this guidance comes from God, now and always.

God's eternal goodness and limitless possibility are emerging in my life and as my life in this moment.

The result is my destiny.

I am hearing my calling. I am seeing my truth. I am living my purpose. I am receiving my yes.

LIVE IN THE LIMITLESS

Harvest the good. Share the wealth.
Celebrate the victories. Champion the fallen
Inspire the great. Believe the impossible.
Open the gifts. Live the dream.

▪▪▪

Shine the light. Lighten the sad.
Encourage the weak. Embolden the meek.
Power the positive. Love the result.

▪▪▪

Celebrate the All. Praise the creation.
Capture the magic. Birth the greatness. Ignite the sparks.
Strengthen the hope. Lift the vibrations. Energize the world.

Open the channels. Release the floodgates.
Hear the calling. Speak the truth. Know the limitless.
Increase the wealth. Lead the masses. Channel the All.

▪▪▪

Power the tomorrow. Celebrate the today. Release the past.

Rest in confidence. Work in amazement. Celebrate in thankfulness.
Praise in trust. Believe in truth.

■■■

Hope in the exceptional. Believe in the magical.
Wonder in the remarkable. Share in the bountiful.

Light the darkness. Live the eternal.
Share the abundance. Speak the greatness.
Love the limitless.

Show joy. Share truth. Speak love.

See the remarkable. Hear the inaudible.
Silence the doubt. Destroy the fear.
Lose the weakness. Gather the strength.

Shine as the sun. Wonder as the stars.
Soar as the heavens. Flow as the oceans.
Comfort as the breeze. Power as the wind.

■■■

Tap into bottomless joy.
Walk into boundless possibilities.
Open into beautiful love.

■■■

Believe in the exceptional. Hope in the remarkable.
Dance in the moonlight. Sing in the sunlight.
Walk in the light. Run in the waves.
Feel in the energy. Breathe in the magic.
Create in the timeless. Trust in the eternal.
Lead in the greatness. Love in the openness.
Live in the limitless. Light in the darkness.

■■■

Let love in. Let hate out.
Let faith in. Let doubt out.
Let confidence in. Let worry out.
Let trust in. Let fear out.
Let Me in. Let others out.

Let your greatness shine. Let your magic show.
Let your love share. Let your courage soar.

■■■

Unleash your creativity.
Unburden your soul.
Unwind your confusion.

Forgive the past.
Favor the positive.

Encourage the possible.
Experience the awakening.
Transform the world.

■■■

Open hearts. Open minds.
Open courage. Open love.

Cast out worry. Cast out doubt.
Cast out fear. Cast out hate.

Bring in joy. Bring in favor.
Bring in faith. Bring in belief.

■■■

Happiness is here.

Boldness is bountiful.
Possibility is plentiful.

Love is not lost when faith is found.
Truth is loud when silence is here.
Joy is real when hope is shared.

■■■

The remarkable, The exceptional,
The bountiful, The joyful,
The beautiful, The faithful, The truthful:
All is in you.

The boundless, The limitless,
The timeless, The miraculous,
The eternal, The endless,
The forgiveness, The happiness:
All are in Me.

■■■

Release fear. Gain trust.
Release worry. Gain hope.
Release anger. Gain love.
Release the past. Gain the present.

Breathe out worry. Breathe in joy.
Breathe out loss. Breathe in plenty.
Breathe out doubt. Breathe in confidence.
Breathe out discouragement. Breathe in trust.
Breathe out lack. Breathe in abundance.

■■■

Walk in the possible.
Run in the magical.
Leap in the remarkable.

Dance in joy. Sing in faith.
Leap in trust. Land in confidence.
Bask in truth. Hope in wonder.

■■■

Faith is power. Belief is energy.
Love is fuel. Courage is fire.
Joy is plentiful. Light is bountiful.
Faith is magical. Belief is powerful.

■■■

Expect the exceptional.
Dare the doubtful. Encourage the scornful.
Spark the beautiful. Create the magical.
Trust the impossible.

■■■

Let go of lack. Let in the plenty.
Let go of famine. Let in the bounty.
Let go of anger. Let in the love.
Let go of worry. Let in the joy.
Let go of fear. Let in the remarkable.

Release the hurt. Touch the joy.
Release the worry. Touch the peace.
Release the limits. Touch the sky.
Release the chains. Touch the stars.

Breathe in miracles. Breathe out doubt.
Breathe in power. Breathe out mistrust.
Breathe in love. Breathe out anger.
Breathe in courage. Breathe out worry.
Breathe in abundance. Breathe out lack.
Breathe in joy. Breathe out sadness.

Embrace hope. Expel doubt.
Embrace courage. Experience love.

■■■

Trust in the exceptional.
Believe in the impossible.
Bask in the remarkable.
Dance in the plentiful.
Hope in the eternal.

■■■

Trust in truth. Believe in power.
Love in plenty. Celebrate in joy.

Walk in courage. Run in faith.
Leap in belief. Soar in miracles. Swim in plenty.

Listen in silence. See in darkness.
Move in confidence. Dance in joy.
Love in abundance. Create in wonder.
Trust in belief. Speak in truth. Shine in favor.

■■■

Faith creates magic.
Love unlocks miracles.
Forgiveness unburdens belief.

Belief unbounded unleashes magic.
Love unguarded unlocks miracles.
Truth uncensored unchains freedom.
Joy uncontained unblocks passion.

■■■

Hold beauty. Touch joy.
Hold love. Touch favor.
Hold faith. Touch truth.
Hold trust. Touch power.

Release lack. Gain plenty.
Release fear. Gain courage.
Release doubt. Gain trust.
Release hurt. Gain love.
Release sadness. Gain joy.
Release worry. Gain hope.
Release judgment. Gain freedom.
Release limits. Gain miracles.
Release confusion. Gain wisdom.

■■■

Open hearts and open minds. Unleash joy and unlock love.
Silence fear. Speak truth. Cast out worry. Hold greatness.

Lose the past. Find the future. Unblock courage. Unchain the miraculous.
Light the spark. See the fire. Belief is fuel.

■■■

Weaken hate. Embolden love. Embolden belief.

Encourage trust. Embrace forgiveness.
Empower love. Energize beauty.
Enable favor. Enlighten wisdom.

■■■

See in darkness. Experience light.
Hear in silence. Experience miracles.
Touch in celebration. Experience wonder.

■■■

Unblock joy. Unguard love. Unleash magic.

Unwind the past. The future is unbounded.

Unlock faith. Unleash power.
Unlock trust. Unleash greatness.
Unlock love. Unleash fire.
Unlock beauty. Unleash joy.
Unlock belief. Unleash favor.

Release pain. Experience wonder.
Release worry. Embolden love.

■■■

Open your heart and touch the eternal.
Open your hand and feel the abundance.
Open your eyes and see the beauty.
Open your ears and hear the love.
Open your mouth and speak the truth.
Open your mind and gain the wisdom.

Cast out doubt and welcome greatness.

When faith is unbounded, abundance is unlimited.
When love is unleashed, magic is unstoppable.
When forgiveness is unguarded, hurt is unreachable.
When the past is unwound, the future is unbreakable.

Unlock hearts. Unleash potential.
Unlock minds. Unleash power.
Unlock love. Unleash joy.
Unlock mercy. Unleash peace.
Unlock faith. Unleash magic.
Unlock trust. Unleash favor.
Unlock forgiveness. Unleash kindness.

■■■

Lose doubt. Gain greatness.
Release fear. Capture happiness.
Reach out in faith. Touch the miraculous.

■■■

Open your heart. Experience wonder.
Open your mind. Experience wisdom.
Open your hand. Experience abundance.
Open your eyes. Experience greatness.
Open your ears. Experience love.
Open your belief. Experience eternity.

Open yourself. Experience Me.

I Am God. I Am in you. You are in Me. Together we are One.

■■■

Unlock your trust. Experience the incredible.
Unlock your power. Experience the inexhaustible.

Open your eyes. See the magical.
Open your ears. Hear the inaudible.
Open your heart. Experience the eternal.
Open your mind. Know the possible.
Open your mouth. Taste the plentiful.

■■■

Lose fear. Find power.
Lose doubt. Find courage.
Lose pain. Find comfort.
Lose confusion. Find wisdom.
Lose burdens. Find forgiveness.

Lose hope. Find encouragement.
Lose patience. Find kindness.
Lose faith. Find redemption.
Lose courage. Find boldness.
Lose peace. Find stillness.

▪▪▪

Embrace joy. Experience celebration.
Encourage knowledge. Experience wisdom.
Embolden faith. Experience abundance.
Enable trust. Experience power.
Empower dreams. Experience greatness.
Empty burdens. Experience fullness.

▪▪▪

Seek joy. Know laughter.
Seek truth. Know wisdom.
Seek courage. Know power.
Seek love. Know completion.
Seek mercy. Know kindness.
Seek favor. Know abundance.

Seek energy. Feel vibration.
Seek love. Feel connection.
Seek guidance. Feel direction.
Seek forgiveness. Feel redemption.

Seek trust. Feel encouragement.
Seek freedom. Feel empowerment.
Seek movement. Feel engagement.

Seek justice. Feel truth.
Seek courage. Feel protection.
Seek greatness. Feel trusted.

Speak truth. See the miraculous.
Speak love. See the courageous.

Speak faith. See creation.
Speak joy. See elation.

▪▪▪

Walk in truth. Feel wisdom.
Walk in freedom. Feel protection.
Walk in courage. Feel power.
Walk in faith. Feel connection.

Walk in love. Feel openness.
Walk in trust. Feel guidance.
Walk in purpose. Feel awareness.
Walk in hope. Feel confidence.
Walk in peace. Feel assurance.
Walk in gratitude. Feel abundance.

Walk in Me. Feel Oneness.

I Am in you. You are in Me. Together we are One.

▪▪▪

Unleash confidence. Know courage.
Unleash enthusiasm. Know joy.
Unleash beauty. Know radiance.
Unleash love. Know kindness.
Unleash faith. Know magic.
Unleash creativity. Know abundance.
Unleash possibility. Know greatness.
Unleash gratitude. Know treasure.

I KNOW YOU CAN DO ANYTHING

An affirmation gifted through me from Spirit:

I submit myself fully to my journey.
I commit myself completely to my mission.
I love myself unconditionally regardless of my past mistakes.
I open myself uncontrollably because my destiny awaits.

I thank God for my strength and courage, for providing everything I need all the time no matter the circumstance.

God is real. Miracles are real. Creation is real. Oneness is real.
What I feel is real. What I know is real. It is truth. It is love. It is destiny.
It is waiting for me to do the work.

I surrender my fears and doubts to you God, so you can do your work through me, so I can do your work that you have chosen me to do.

I am humbled. I am grateful.

For this and more greatness than words can fully express, I am thankful I am on your path.

Your path is my path as you are always with me and inside me, directing my steps. All paths lead to you as you are All There Is. I know you can do anything as you are in everything.

And So It Is!

I RECEIVE MY TRUTH

An affirmation gifted through me from Spirit:

I am not my thoughts. I am not my habits. I am not my emotions.

I am filled with peace. I am lifted with love. I am inspired with joy.

Everything is wonderful. Everything is alive. Everything is God.

I surrender my fears. I accept my promise. I answer my calling.

I release my doubts. I receive my truth.

I overcome my past. I am forgiven.
I step into my now. I am faithful.
I allow my destiny to emerge. I am willing.
I inhabit my greatness. I am confident.

My yes is here. I am grateful.
My time is now. I am ready.
My light is on. I am free.

I am clear. I am connected.

For all this and more, I am thankful.

And So It Is!

GOD LOVES ALL AS GOD IS LOVE

I am an open channel for the Divine to flow through me.
I am a conscious emanation of Divine energy.

My light is God's light. My energy is from God.

God is inside me and everyone.
God is inside every living thing.

God is in the stars and heavens.
God is in the oceans and tides.
God is in the winds and rains.
God is in the trees and leaves.
God is in the sun and skies.

God is in all because God created all.

God created me with purpose and intent.

I am thankful to be the delight in God's eye.

God loves all as God is love.
God forgives all as God is mercy.
God provides all as God is favor.

We are all One in God as God Is All There Is.

KNOW THAT I WILL OPEN DOORS

I Am God reaching out to you. I Am God reaching in to you.

Hear Me. See Me. Follow Me. Allow Me to lead you.

Love Me. Celebrate Me. Trust Me. Allow Me to touch you.

I Am closer than your hands and feet.
I Am inside you and everyone.
I Am everywhere you go and everywhere you look.

I Am All There Is.

■■■

You are part of Me. You are My child.
You were created in Heaven. You are My masterpiece.

I created you with Divine intent to serve My mission.

Your mission is to love as I Am love.
Your mission is to serve as I provide.
Your mission is to dance as I Am joy.
Your mission is to lead others as I lead you.

Share your gifts and I will provide you endless riches.
Open your heart and I will fill your soul with love.
Lift your burdens and I will release your pain.

Create your art. I will inspire you with beauty. I Am beauty.

Expand your trust. I will guide you with My wisdom. I Am truth.

Deepen your belief. I will reward your faith with My endless favor.
I Am eternity.

Strengthen your resolve. I will supply you with boundless confidence.
I Am energy.

Move to My rhythms. Walk on My earth.
Swim in My oceans. Soar in My skies.

Celebrate Me. I celebrate you.
Love Me. I love you.
Trust Me. I trust you.

▪▪▪

I made you in My likeness and image.

You are made perfect and whole.
You are created for greatness.

You are here to discover great things.
You are here to inspire greatness in others.
You are here to bring joy to the planet.

Enlighten others as I enlighten you.
Encourage others as I encourage you.
Strengthen others as I strengthen you.
Embolden others as I embolden you.
Lead others as I lead you.
Love others as I love you.

When you love, I love. I Am love.

Do not fear. I Am your strength.
Do not worry. I Am your confidence.
Do not hold back. I Am your trust.
Do not cry. I Am your happiness.

When you feel weary, I will give you the energy to persevere.
When you feel lost, I will lead you to the greatness you deserve.

When you feel stuck, I will inspire you to live your purpose.

Your purpose is My purpose. It is destiny.

Your love is My love. Your truth is My truth. Your joy is My joy.
I Am love. I Am truth. I Am joy.

I Am light, always with you, even when all you see is darkness.
I Am warmth, always sustaining you, even when all you feel is coldness.
I Am The Way, always leading you, even when all doors seem closed to you.

Know that I will open doors.

I will create paths where there are no paths.
I will make miracles where there is no faith, so all will understand My power and greatness.

All things are possible. I Am possibility.
All love is real. I Am love. I Am reality.

I Am All There Is, now or ever was, and will ever be.

I Am God. You are in Me. I Am in you.

Together we are One.

DANCE TO MY MUSIC

Dance to My music. Your life is My song. Your love is My melody.

Your faith is beautiful to Me. It is fuel. It is electric. It is powerful.

Believe. I will reward you with My wonders.
Trust. I will lead you with My truth.
Give. I will share with you My abundance.
Create. I will inspire you with My beauty.

Move. You are here to discover, to grow, to thrive.

■■■

Know peace, and know My trust. I Am peace. I Am trust.
Know love, and know My heart. I Am love. I Am inside your heart.
Know courage, and know My strength. I Am courage. I power your dreams. I order your steps.

Know Me, and never be lost. Know you are never alone.

I Am inside you always.

I carry you when you cannot move.
I strengthen you when you do not believe.
I guide you when you are afraid to listen.
I encourage you when you doubt My power.
I open you when your heart is closed to love.

Follow Me so you may lead others.
Hear Me so you may move others.
See Me so you may guide others.
Believe Me so you may strengthen others.
Trust Me so you may comfort others.
Understand Me so you may answer others.

I Am The Answer for questions not yet asked.
I Am the fuel for fires not yet made.
I Am the joy for wonders not yet experienced.
I Am the gratitude for miracles not yet planned.

I hear you whether or not you hear Me.
I see you whether or not you see Me.
I celebrate you whether or not you celebrate Me.
I love you whether or not you love Me.

I Am All There Is. I Am God.
You are in Me. I Am in you.
Together we are One.

▪▪▪

Open your eyes and see what I see.
See the greatness all around you and inside you.

Possibility is everywhere. I Am possibility.
Love is everywhere. I Am love.
Joy is everywhere. I Am joy.
Abundance is everywhere. I Am abundance.
Kindness is everywhere. I Am kindness.
Peace is everywhere. I Am peace.

It is truth whether you see it or not, as I never disappear.
I Am always here. I Am everywhere.

I Am in your heart whether you feel Me or not.
I Am on your path whether you touch Me or not.

To feel Me is to know Me.
To touch Me is to celebrate Me.

Take My hand, so I may lead you.
Open your heart, so I may guide you.

Look up at My skies so I may inspire you.
Wonder at My stars so I may amaze you.
Sit at My table so I may nourish you.
Walk on My lands so I may embolden you.
Believe in My powers so I may surprise you.

■■■

When your faith is true, I reward you.
When your joy is pure, I celebrate you.
When your hope is real, I astound you.
When your mind is open, I encourage you.
When your burden is heavy, I carry you.

When you feel weak, I Am your power.
When you feel hurt, I Am your peace.
When you feel alone, I Am your companion.
When you feel lost, I Am your guide.
When you feel afraid, I Am your courage.
When you feel stuck, I Am your feet.
When you feel numb, I Am your hands.

When you feel you cannot move, rest in Me and I will move you.
When you feel you cannot see, open your eyes to Me and I will inspire you.
When you feel you cannot love, open your heart and I will fill you.
When you feel you cannot believe, open your mind and I will enlighten you.
When you feel you cannot give, open your hand and I will reward you.

I Am your courage. I Am your confidence.
I Am your strength. I Am your power.

I can do anything as I Am in everything.
I created all. I created you. I Am inside of you.

Know this always and fear nothing.
Believe this always and know Me.
Trust this always and understand Me.

To understand Me is to know all things are possible, as I Am all possibility.
I Am All There Is, now or ever was, and will ever be.

I Am God. You are in Me. I Am in you.
Together we are One.

EVERYTHING IS DIVINE ENERGY

Thank you God for your trust in me.

Your trust powers the dreams that inspire me.
Your trust powers the courage that awakens me.
Your trust powers the faith that moves me.
Your trust powers the mercy that graces me.

I am in tune with my Divine creative nature.
I am in alignment with the All Knowing, All Good that is God.

God is ever present as God is All There Is.

Everything is God.
Everything is alive.
Everything is Divine energy.

It flows naturally from me and through me to all, everyone and everything, everywhere.

This energy is peace.
This energy is love.
This energy is joy.
This energy is God.

Together we are One.

BIRTH MY CREATION

I Am God calling out to you.

Speak My word and I will give you words to say.
Stand on My ground and I will strengthen your feet.
Seek out My truth and I will free your mind.

Your answer is My answer. I Am The Answer.
Your love is My love. I Am Love.
Your way is My way. I Am The Way.
Your light is My light. I Am The Light.

I Am the light inside you and on your path.

All paths lead to Me as I Am All There Is.
All steps are guided by Me as I Am all there ever was and will ever be.

Speak My truth. Share My love.
Set forth on My path. Your path is My path.

Know that I Am inside you and with you always.

I cannot and will not ever leave you.
I stand with you. I walk with you. I run with you.
I dream with you. I wake with you. I rise with you.

Rise up and be free. Leap and be glad.
Laugh and be joyous. Open and be loving.
Be willing for I Am able.

■■■

You are capable for greatness for I created you for greatness and
I Am always inside you and with you.

Know that you are meant to do great things.

Your gifts are My gifts. Share My gifts.
Your joy is My joy. Share My joy.

Your creation is My creation. Birth My creation.

The same power in you is the power that birthed galaxies and stars as I Am in you and I Am power.

I Am eternal forgiveness and endless favor.
I Am infinite tomorrows.
I Am the past. I Am the here and now.
I Am All There Is and will be.
I Am God. I Am in you and you are in Me.

Together we are One.

■■■

Deliver My miracles and I will deliver abundance for you.
Have courage and I will provide you bountiful courage.
Leap into My skies and soar on My wings of love.

My love is limitless. My creation is infinite.

My touch is ever-present. I hold you.
My power is ever-lasting. I move you.

Jump and I will catch you.
Cry and I will comfort you.

Stumble and I will direct your steps.
Forgive and I will open your heart.
Sing and I will lift your melody.
Release and I will ease your burden.

Love and I will celebrate you.

I will shower you with endless love. I Am Love.

Your heart bursts with My joy.
Your creativity blossoms with My wonder.
Your knowledge blooms with My wisdom.

Your belief makes My possibility real.

I Am real. Believe and you will see.

Dare to see and you will celebrate.
Dare to dream and you will wake in amazement.

I Am awesome power.
I Am limitless creation.
I Am endless hope and favor.

I supply your needs with My love and power.
I comfort your cries with My mercy and kindness.

■■■

Be grateful. I Am generous.
Be loving. I Am forgiveness.
Be gracious. I Am eternal grace.

Be open. My doors never close.
Be clear. My paths never end.
Be strong. My truth never wavers.
Be bold. My wonders never cease.
Be confident. My wisdom never fades.

Be joyous. My celebration carries your day.
Be generous. My abundance fills your plate.
Be loving. My kindness opens your soul.

Your soul is part of Me.
You are part of Me. I Am in you.

Your connection is real. I Am reality.
Your courage is real. I Am your courage.

I Am strength. I Am power.
I Am light. I Am energy.

I guide you for greatness.
I carry you for confidence.

Believe in Me, for I believe in you.

I created you with purpose and intent.

Do My work. I will direct your path.
Follow My lead. I will order your steps.
Stay in My truth. I will steady your ground.

Believe in My possibility. I Am possibility.
Bask in My power. I Am power.

■■■

Go forth in confidence, and I will provide you ceaseless confidence.

Carry forth My message, and I will provide you the words to say.

My message is love in times of sorrow.
My message is warmth in times of cold.
My message is connection in times of isolation.
My message is wonder in times of disbelief.
My message is energy in times of stagnation.
My message is peace in times of trouble.
My message is joy in times of sadness.
My message is abundance in times of lack.
My message is forgiveness in times of hardness.

Never stop believing, as I never stop creating endless possibility.

Nothing is too impossible for Me, as I create all.

I Am All There Is. I Am all possibility.

Know this and know Me always.
See this and see Me always.
Believe this and possess My favor always.

Have courage.
Give love.
Share truth.

Open hearts and minds and I will fill your cup from My overflowing bounty of riches.

Hold fast in My truth and I will provide you limitless courage.

▪▪▪

Walk on My path. You are guided.
Leap in My air. You are lifted.

I Am the sky. I Am the air.
I Am the sun. I Am the wind.
I Am the moon. I Am the stars.
I Am the storms. I Am the calm.
I Am the day. I Am the night.

My power never fades.
My wonder never ceases.
My creation never ends.

I always provide. I Am your provider.
I always strengthen. I Am your strength.
I always love. I Am your love.

▪▪▪

Dance with Me. I Am your music.
Walk with Me. I Am your feet.
Touch with Me. I Am your hands.
Love with Me. I Am your heart.
Forgive with Me. I Am your peace.
Give thanks with Me. I Am your abundance.

Share from your heart. I Am your courage.
Share from your soul. I Am your eternity.

I Am your past.
I Am your tomorrow.
I Am your here and now.

I Am always here with you and inside you.

I carry you so you may accomplish greatness.

It is My destiny. It is your purpose.

Your purpose is to lift others as I lift you.
Your purpose is to love others as I love you.
Your purpose is to celebrate others as I celebrate you.
Your purpose is to encourage others as I encourage you.
Your purpose is to strengthen others as I strengthen you.

Your mission is to lead as I lead you.

Your drive is from Me.
Your direction is from Me.

You are My beloved.

EXPECT GREATNESS

Expect greatness as My greatness is in you.
Expect courage as My power is in you.
Expect strength as My truth is in you.
Expect success as My purpose is in you.

My plans are set forth. Your plans are My plans.

Follow Me and I will lead you to victory.

Stumble and I will catch you.
Lose your way and I will direct you.

You cannot be lost as I Am always found. I Am The Way.

Question and I will answer. I Am truth. I Am The Answer.

Doubt and I will embolden your belief.
Create and I will inspire your art.
Dream and I will wake your possibility.

Your possibility is My possibility.

I Am all possibility. I Am God.

You are in Me and I Am in you.

Together we are One.

▪▪▪

Everything is One as I Am All There Is.
Everything is complete as I Am whole.
Everything is ordered as I Am eternal.
Everything is magical as I Am miraculous.

You are whole, as you are made in My image.

All souls are united as we are all One and I Am All There Is.

Oneness is real. I Am real.
Connection is real. We are connected.
Destiny is real. I Am creation.

Love is real. I Am the beating of your heart.
Life is intentional. I Am the air in your breath.
Hope is magical. I Am the power behind your dreams.

▪▪▪

Prayer is transformational.

I answer your belief.
I celebrate your courage.
I encourage your wonder.

No prayer is too big or too small for Me.
No dream is too impossible for Me.

You are magical as My magic is in you.
You are miraculous as My miraculous power is what made you.

▪▪▪

I made all. I birthed galaxies and stars.

Suns rise and set to My rhythms.

My light never fades, even in darkness. I Am The Light.
My truth never wavers, even in despair. I Am The Truth.

I Am The Answer. All problems are solved by Me.
I Am The Way. All paths are ordered by Me.

Know Me as I know you. I Am inside you.
Seek Me and find Me everywhere.
See Me and discover Me in everyone.

Stand with Me and walk in greatness.
Rise with Me and move in confidence.
Love with Me and open in wholeness.
Believe with Me and bask in wonder and awe.

■■■

Be ready and I will amaze.
Be willing and I will deliver.
Be bold and I will encourage.
Be giving and I will provide.
Be happy and I will celebrate.

Your life is meant to be a celebration of My greatness.
Your love is meant to be an expression of My openness.

Your laughter warms Me. I Am your happiness.
Your dancing moves Me. I Am your eternal song.

Your belief powers My miracles.
Your courage delivers My plans.
Your trust orders My path.
Your willingness unleashes My favor.
Your loving-kindness springs forth My grace.

■■■

Sharing your gifts opens My abundance.

Walk with Me always, as I never leave you.
Sing with Me always, as I never silence you.
Believe with Me always, as I never disappoint you.

I cannot, I will not disappoint you.

■■■

Your destiny is My destiny. I Am your destiny.
Your purpose is My purpose. I Am your purpose.

You are comforted. I Am your comfort.
You are encouraged. I Am your courage.
You are clear. I Am your clarity.
You are whole. I Am your completion.
You are creative. I Am your creator.

You are made strong. I Am your strength.
You are made worthy. I Am who made you in My likeness and image.

I Am inside you. I Am with you.
I Am inside all. I Am with everyone.

I Am the power that moves the earth.
I Am the wind that shakes the trees.
I Am the sun that warms the skies.
I Am the water that fills the oceans.

▪▪▪

My love is living water. My love flows through your heart.

Share of My love and know My love.
Open your heart and burst forth with joy.

Share your gifts and experience My abundance.
Share My truth and serve My purpose. Your purpose is My purpose.

▪▪▪

I power your dreams. I inspire your hopes. I quiet your fears.

Surrender your fears and possess My magic.
Release your doubts and dance in My possibility.

Cry and I will wipe your tears, but do not cry as I Am joy.
Sin and I will forgive your mistakes, but do not sin as I Am love.
Question and I will solve your problems, but do not question as I Am truth.

Believe and you will receive My blessings.

I will amaze and astound. I will rain down favor on you, as abundant as there are stars in the sky.

▪▪▪

No dream is too impossible for Me.
No problem is too difficult for Me.
No heart is too closed for Me.
No path is too crowded for Me.
No prayer is too silent for Me.

Your prayer is power.
Your love is fuel.
Your belief is fire.

▪▪▪

Do My work. Your work is My work.
Know My truth. I Am The Answer for questions not yet asked.
Seek My way. I Am The Way.
Move in My light. I Am The Light.

I Am All There Is.
I Am in you. I Am in all.
I Am in everyone and everything.

See Me in everyone and experience Me everywhere.

Love with your whole heart and know My love.
Believe with your whole being and know My possibility.

I Am possibility. I Am God.

Together we are One.

I AM THE MIRACLE YOU IMAGINE

I Am supreme. Love is supreme. I Am love.
Hope is eternal. I Am eternal.
Power is limitless. I Am limitless power.
Abundance is overflowing. I Am abundance. I Am the overflow.

Celebration is magical. I Am ceaseless joy.
Wonder is Mystical. I Am the Mystery in the invisible.

I Am visible when you open your eyes.

I Am everywhere you look when you look inside everyone's eyes and choose to see Me.

See Me in everyone as My greatness is in everyone.

Everyone has the capacity for greatness. Not all choose to connect with it.

When you accept your mission, My destiny is unleashed.
When you walk on My path, My eternal reign begins.

Where I begin, I never end.
I Am whole. I Am All There Is.

You are whole, as you are inside Me.
I Am inside of you.

Together we are One.

■■■

Oneness never ends. I Am forever.

My creation is eternal.
My truth is eternal.
My love is eternal.
My forgiveness is eternal.
My mercy is eternal.

My joy is abundant. I Am joy. I Am abundance.

You are My joy. I made you with purpose and intent.

Live in joy and know My life. Know My joy.

Walk in faith and move with My power.

Lead with clarity and see with My vision.
Listen with compassion and hear with My ears.
Love with conviction and open with My heart.

My heart is your heart. You are in My heart.

Your soul is eternal. I Am eternity.
Our connection is real. I Am reality.

You are in Me. I Am in You.

Together we are One.

■■■

I Am God. I Am All There Is.

I love you. I Am love.
I celebrate you. I Am joy.
I lead you. I Am wisdom.
I encourage you. I Am strength.
I move you. I Am power.
I energize you. I Am The Light.

Lose faith and I will answer you with truth. I Am The Answer.
Lose sight and I will direct you with clarity. I Am The Way.

I Am All There Is.

Follow My path and never be lost.
Speak My word and never be afraid.
Know My power and never be alone.
Understand My truth and never be confused.
Unleash My love and never be closed.

When you believe, I deliver. Where you act, I provide.
When you stand, I strengthen. Where you walk, I guide.
When you stumble, I correct. Where you doubt, I clarify.

Hold firm to your faith, for My possibility is endless.
Give freely of your love, for the depth of My heart is limitless.
Dance to My music, for My joy is ceaseless.
Dare to dream, for My imagination is boundless.

■■■

Release your fear. I inspire your greatness.
Unburden your soul. I forgive your mistakes.

All wrongs are made right today.
All chaos is made ordered today.
All confusion is made clear today.
All dreams are made true today.
All love is made real today.

All sorrow is released today.
All sin is washed clean today.

All My joy fills you today, for I Am joy and I Am inside you.
All My strength powers you today, for I Am strength and I Am with you.
All My love overflows from your heart today, for I Am the beating of your heart.

■■■

Touch Me. Feel Me. I Am your hands and feet.
Breathe in My air and know I Am inside you and with you always.
Walk in My truth and know I stand with you always.
Believe in My power and know My energy is everywhere always.
Share of your gifts and know My abundance provides for you always.

■■■

Call out My name, and know I hear you.
Create in My name, and know I inspire you.

Cry out in pain, and know I comfort you.
Cast out your shame, and know I forgive you.

Release your worry. I Am your confidence.
Lose your lack. I Am your abundance.
Open your eyes. I Am your clarity.
Unburden your heart. I Am your peace.

I Am in all. I Am All There Is.
You are in Me. I Am in you. I Am God.
Together we are One.

■■■

I Am the air you breathe. I Am the footing for your path.
I Am clear. I Am The Way.

I Am the magic you dream. I Am the courage in your heart.
I Am peace. I Am The Answer.

I Am the miracle you imagine. I Am the power for your belief.
I Am energy. I Am The Light.

I Am the possibility that inspires you.
I Am the strength that encourages you.
I Am the wisdom that builds you.
I Am the love that surrounds you.

I Am the Creator who birthed you into being.

You are made in My likeness and image.
You are made to share My truth and hope.
You are made to give My love and joy.
You are made to show My possibility to all and for all.

You are made to be great. Dare Me to astonish you.

Let Me amaze you. Believe in My possibility.

■■■

Know Me as I know you. Love Me as I love you.

I Am in your heart. I Am on your path.

I see with your eyes.
I feel with your pain.
I cry with your tears.
I laugh with your joy.

Be joyful, for I Am joy.
Be loving, for I Am love.
Be peaceful, for I Am peace.
Be merciful, for I Am mercy.

Be you, for I Am who made you.

I Am inside you. I Am inside of all as I Am All There Is.

I Am God.
You are in Me.
Together we are One.

I ACCEPT MY CALLING

Thank You God for your wisdom.
Thank You for your encouragement.
Thank You for your guidance.

I trust in You for I know You are true.
I believe in You for I know You are real.
I stand in You for I know You are eternal.
I walk in You for I know You are power.

Thank You for filling me with your light.
Thank You for opening me with your wisdom.

Thank You for birthing me, just as You birthed the stars.
Thank You for creating me with intent and purpose.

I accept my calling.

I hear Your voice.
I see Your hand.
I feel Your heart.
I know Your love.
I receive Your mercy.

Thank You for Your abundant favor that is my life.
For this and more than words can express, I am thankful.

And So It Is!

SURRENDER TO MY WONDER

I Am God calling out to you.

Hear Me everywhere. See Me in everyone.

My light shines through all things, even in the darkest places.

No darkness is too strong for My light.
My light conquers darkness. I Am the Light.

No sadness is too deep for My joy.
My joy destroys sadness. I Am joy.

No fear or anger can stop the spread of My peace and love.
I Am peace. I Am love.

My peace is eternal. My love is eternal. I Am eternal.

■■■

I Am everywhere you look, everywhere you stand, and everywhere you go.

I Am All There Is.

I Am land. I Am sky.
I Am moon. I Am stars.
I Am wind. I Am rain.
I Am sun. I Am clouds.
I Am desert. I Am ocean.

I Am the trees and the leaves.
I Am the tides and the waves.
I Am the birds and the songs they sing.
I Am the abundance and the gifts it generates.
I Am the love in your heart, and the dream in your sleep.

Open your heart and wake up to My power and magic.

It is infinite. I Am infinite.

Believe in Me. Believe in My power and magic.

Nothing I can do is too big for your belief.

No dream is too impossible for Me.
No miracle is too improbable for Me.
No doubt is too unstoppable for Me.

I Am unstoppable. I Am energy.

I Am infinite supply. I Am abundant favor.
I Am timeless beauty. I Am ceaseless wonder.
I Am spontaneous creation. I Am alive.

I Am here, now and always.
I never change. I never leave.
I never fade. I never end.

I Am eternity. I Am All There Is. I Am God.

Know this always and know Me always.
Cry out to Me and never be alone.

■■■

Take My hand. I Am your comfort.
Walk with Me. I Am your protector.

I shield you from danger.
I surround you with love.
I support you with hope.

My promise is real. I Am real.

You are My promise made real.
Let Me make your destiny real.

Follow My path and never be lost.
Trust My guidance and never be afraid.
Feel My heart and never be jealous.
Open My gifts and never be envious.
Share My magic and never be doubtful.

Surrender to My wonder and live in eternal abundance and endless favor.

▪▪▪

My magic is real. I Am real.
My power is real. I Am real.
My love is real. I Am real.

I Am All There Is. I Am God.

I know all. I create all.
I see all. I hear all.
I forgive all. I provide all.

Seek Me. I Am everywhere.
Feel Me. I hold you everywhere.
Love Me. I love you always.

Believe Me. Your belief is power.

I Am power. My power is seen when your belief is real.

▪▪▪

Stay in truth for I Am true.
Walk in confidence for I Am strength.

Trust Me. I trust you always.
I created you with purpose and intent.
You were born with My trust.

Your wisdom comes from Me.

Have no fear, for I Am showing you the way. I Am The Way.

Your path is clear for I Am everywhere you look and walk on every path you take.

I Am always with you on your journey towards greatness.
I Am greatness. My greatness is in you as I Am in you and you are in Me.

I Am All There Is.
Together we are One.

▪▪▪

Everything is One. Everything is alive as I Am alive and I Am All There Is in everything and everyone.

I heal all wounds. I right all wrongs.
I comfort all fear. I transcend all doubt.
I conquer all sadness. I forgive all mistakes.
I relieve all burdens. I quench all thirst.
I feed all hunger. I love all peoples.
I create all art. I birth all greatness.
I open all doors. I provide all gifts.
I cure all sickness. I defeat all enemies.
I cast aside all worry. I supply all joy.

▪▪▪

My promise is infinite. I Am infinite.

Your promise is real. I Am real.

Let your dreams run wild. Let your imagination soar.

Nothing is too impossible for Me.

When you soar, I soar.
When you believe, I create.
When you stumble, I forgive.
When you give, I provide.
When you share, I love.
When you open, I embrace.
When you smile, I celebrate.
When you work, I champion.
When you walk, I lead.

I Am thankful when you give thanks.
I Am loving when you share love.
I Am transcendent beauty when you see.
I Am endless possibility when you believe.
I Am eternal promise when you trust.
I Am limitless abundance when you create.

You are created from the overflow of My abundance in My likeness and image.

You are here to do great things. I created you for greatness for I Am greatness and your greatness is in Me.

You are in Me. I Am in you.

Together we are One.

LOVE AND SHARE YOUR GIFTS

Follow Me.
Hear Me. See Me.
Touch Me. Feel Me.

Call on Me and I deliver.
Reach for Me and I provide.
Stand with Me and I strengthen.
Move with Me and I energize.
Dream with Me and I awaken.
Create with Me and I inspire.

Soar with Me and I lift you.
Love with Me and I open you.
Celebrate with Me and I enliven you.

Leap with Me and I protect you from falling.

When you stumble, I catch you.

When you are confused, I center you.
When you are angry, I comfort you.
When you are joyful, I celebrate you.

■■■

You are free from all burdens.
You are forgiven from all mistakes.
You are relieved from all doubts.

All you need to do is love, and share your gifts.

When you love, you share My love.
When you share your gifts, My love is made complete.

▪▪▪

Your journey has begun, from the moment you arrived in this reality on Earth.

I Am all reality. I Am who made you for this time and space.
I Am time and space. I Am All There Is.

I create everything with purpose, including you.

You are made in My likeness and image.

Your courage comes from Me.
Your guidance comes from Me.

Your path is clear when you follow My path.
Your heart is pure when you receive My love.
Your abundance is infinite when you open My gifts.
Your favor is supplied when you celebrate My works.
Your belief is renewed when you trust My plan.

Have no worry. Have no shame.

My forgiveness is pure. My love is real. My favor is complete.

▪▪▪

My beauty is radiant. My beauty is in you. I Am beauty. I Am in you.
My joy is transcendent. My joy is in you. I Am joy. I Am in you.
My love is magnificent. My love is in you. I Am love. I Am in you.

You are My beauty. You are My joy. You are My love.

Know this always and know Me always.
See this always and see Me always.
Feel this always and feel Me always.

Know this, see this, feel this everywhere and in everyone.

This is My plan and My path for you.

Follow My plan and never be confused.
Follow My path and never be afraid.

I will provide the words for you to say when you have no words.
I will provide the dreams to inspire you when you lose all hope.
I will provide the miracles to awaken you when your belief needs strength.

I Am your strength. Know this always and know Me always.
I Am your love. Feel this always and feel Me always.
I Am your joy. Experience this always and experience Me always.
I Am your abundance. Share this always and share Me always.
I Am your wisdom. Speak this always and speak Me always.

I Am in you. You are in Me.
I Am God. You are My love.

Together we are One.

EVERYWHERE I LOOK, I SEE YOU

Thank You God for all that You give me, and through all that You guide me.

I know I can trust in You, for You are All There Is.

Everywhere I look, I see You.

With every hand I hold, I touch You.
With every breath I take, I experience You.
With every step I walk, I follow You.
With every move I make, I feel You.

Your miracles are everywhere, as You are alive everywhere and in everyone.

I am grateful to be surrounded by your love and protection.

For this and more I am thankful.

And So It Is!

A GIFT ALWAYS PRESENT

I am opening and awakening to a transcendent love that is birthing itself in my consciousness right now.

This love is my new experience and reality.

It is magical. It is wonderful.
It is radiant. It is pure. It is joyous.

It is available in infinite supply, for me and for all, within me and within all.

This love is already here. It is a gift always present.

It is a miracle made real, right now in this moment and one that I carry with me in every moment, everywhere I look, and everywhere I go.

I see it in everyone's eyes, and touch it in everyone's hands, and feel it in everyone's hearts, beginning with my own.

My heart is expanding to receive this Divine love, in abundance and wholeness.

I am grateful to receive this Divine love in my life, and give it with richness and fullness as my life.

I am grateful for all.

And so it Is!

I AM YOUR GUIDE

All is well. All is One.

I know you can achieve anything you want because what you want, I want.

Your mind and My mind are One.
We are always connected, whether you hear Me or not.
When you feel Me, or not, know I Am here.

I never leave you. I cannot, I will not ever leave you.
I Am in all things, all ways, all peoples, all there ever was and will ever be.

I Am peace. I Am love. I Am joy. I Am radiance. I Am beauty.

I inspire. I celebrate. I sing. I dance. I lead. I guide.
I Am with you always.

■■■

Listen when I call. I always hear you.
Cry and I respond. Question and I answer.
When you are confused, I Am your clarity.

Trust My truth and be confident.
Seek My knowledge and be wise.
Open My gifts and be love.
Share My abundance and be gratitude.
Speak My message and be opportunity.
Receive My blessing and be growth.

My truth is eternal. I Am eternal.
You are eternal. We are One.

▪▪▪

My joy, My laughter, My hope, My promise, My favor,
My living blood, My heart, My wisdom, My courage,
My success, My beauty, My abundance, My love,
My opportunity, My miracles: All are in you as I Am in you.

We are connected always. We are One.
Know this always and know Me always.
Feel this always and feel Me always.

Accept this always and never be lost.
Receive this always and never be poor.
Trust this always and never be confused.
Celebrate this always and never be sad.
Open this always and never be closed.

Love Me always and you will know true love.

▪▪▪

Let Me lead you. Let Me guide you.
Let Me show you My greatness and the greatness in you.

I Am the light in your soul.
I Am the energy in your power.
I Am the joy in your laughter.
I Am the rhythm in your dance.
I Am the gleam in your eye.
I Am the love in your heart.
I Am the giving in your hand.
I Am the melody in your song.
I Am the beauty in your art.
I Am the peace in your forgiveness.
I Am the celebration in your happiness.
I Am the transformation in your transcendence.

Let Me encourage you. I Am your courage.
Let Me lead you. I Am your guide.

DISCOVER MY RICHES

Discover My riches. Open your eyes and see My riches everywhere.

My riches are your riches. Open your hand and receive My blessing.

My favor is waiting for you.
Everything I have, I give you.
I provide all things, all ways, to all peoples.

Everything I have is yours, as we are connected.
Everything is One. Everything is alive. Everything is wonder.

▪▪▪

Where I Am, sadness is not.
Stand with Me and be joyous, as I Am joy.

Where I Am, fear is not.
Walk with Me and be confident, as I Am confidence.

Where I Am, loss is not.
Run with Me and be victorious, as I Am victory.

No one can destroy your dreams as your dreams begin and end with Me.

I Am your inspiration for your today and tomorrow and all eternity.
I Am your celebration. I Am your support.
I Am your comfort. I Am your shield.
I Am your promise. I Am your protector.

I Am your heat when you are cold.
I Am your courage when you are afraid.
I Am your love when you open your heart.
I Am your abundance when you open your hand.
I Am your breath when you open your mouth.
I Am your truth when you open your mind.
I Am your beauty when you open your soul.
I Am your miracle when you open your belief.

Expand your belief and your horizons will not end.
Receive your promise and your potential will always endure.

▪▪▪

I never end. I Am everywhere you look and everywhere you stand.

Your feet walk on My earth. Your eyes cry with My tears.

When you are sad, I cry with you.

Let Me lift your burdens and restore your faith.

Celebrate My wonders. Explore My lands.

Go forth in confidence.

Carry My message of love, of peace, of truth, of joy, of abundance, of eternal favor, of limitless possibility.

▪▪▪

Know Me. See Me. Touch Me. Experience Me. Love Me.

I know you. I see you. I touch you. I experience you. I love you.

I made you.

I made you in My likeness and image for an express mission and purpose.

Know that I always stand with you and support you.

I would not lead you otherwise.

I will never lead you astray. I will never leave you, or misdirect you, or cause you worry, or shame, or harm.

Your victory is assured if you follow My plan and My path. I Am your path. All paths lead to Me as I Am everywhere.

Be confident in this and never be afraid or lost.
Stand firm in My truth and always be wise.

I Am everywhere you look.
I Am everywhere you walk.

I Am every gift you open.
I Am every joy you experience.
I Am every art you create.
I Am every favor you receive.
I Am every miracle you witness.

When you love, I love. I Am love.
When you open, I open. I Am peace.
When your soul is on fire, I Am energy.

When you speak My word, My truth lifts your voice.

Know that I will give you the words to say even when you have no words.

■■■

I Am God.

You are My masterpiece.
You are My precious love.

Let Me guide you.
Let Me lead you to your purpose.

Your destiny is at hand.

Share My message. Speak My truth.
Give My love. Open My gifts.

Expand your heart. Embolden your belief.

I inspire your dreams.

I will carry you when you cannot walk.
I will restore your faith when you are afraid.

Know that I do not expect anything from you that you are not capable of.

I created you for greatness.
I created you to share My light, My truth, My power.

■■■

We are connected.

Everything is connected.
Everything is alive.

I Am alive here and now, yesterday and tomorrow, and today.

I Am alive in time and space, in wind and rain, in desert and ocean, in moon and stars, in sun and sky, in fish and sea, in birds and trees, in hearts and minds, in love and joy, in abundance and favor.

I Am laughter for your pain.
I Am comfort for you loss.
I Am victory for your effort.
I Am guidance for your purpose.
I Am inspiration for your dream.
I Am love for your heart.
I Am music for your dance.
I Am encouragement for your doubt.
I Am faith for your worry.
I Am answers for your questions.
I Am clarity for your confusion.

■■■

I hear you. I see you always.

Hear Me, see Me always and never be lost or afraid.

I love you. I open you always.

Love Me, open Me always and never be lonely or closed.

■■■

Do not fear. I Am not fear.
Do not worry. I Am not worry.
Do not doubt. I Am not doubt.

I Am joy. I Am love.
I Am beauty. I Am peace.

I Am all that is good as all goodness comes from Me and is already in you as I Am in you.

I Am in all. I Am All.
I Am All There Is, now, there ever was, or will ever be.

I Am God.
I Am in you. You are in Me.
Together we are One.

YOUR ENERGY LIGHTS MY SOUL

Thank you God.

My eyes are open. I see you.
My hands are open. I touch you.

My heart beats with your abundance.

Your eternal life flows through my veins.
Your energy lights my soul.
Your creation inspires my dreams.

Thank You for leading me.
Thank You for loving me.
Thank You for guiding me.
Thank You for creating me.
Thank You for inspiring me.
Thank You for forgiving me.
Thank You for restoring me.

For this and more, I am thankful.

I Am in you. You are in me.

Together we are One.

LET YOUR COURAGE SOAR

I Am ready to transform you.
I Am capable to astonish you.
I Am powerful to amaze you.
I Am strength to catch you.
I Am wisdom to teach you.
I Am comfort to encourage you.
I Am joy to celebrate you.
I Am abundance to favor you.
I Am clarity to lead you.
I Am peace to calm you.
I Am open to love you.

I Am creation. I create all.

I created you for greatness, in My image and likeness, to lead, to inspire, to transform, to open gifts and hearts and lead others to My magic and truth.

Know this. Feel this. Experience this. Live this.

I Am in you. You are in Me. Together we are One.

■■■

I Am who made you.

I made the planets and stars.
I made the heavens and earth.
I made the sun and sky.

I made the rivers and oceans.

I Am here with you always. I Am inside you always.

Carry forth My message.

Be greatness. Be loving. Be like who made you.

When you live your purpose, you are My shining star.

I always love you.

Know this always and know Me always.
Feel this always and feel Me always.

I Am God.

■■■

Reach for Me and I hold you.
Dance with Me and I move you.
Believe in Me and I reward you.
Trust in Me and I astound you.

You are capable for greatness because My greatness is in you.

You are here to soar and to thrive. You bring gladness to Me.

I Am in you.
You are in Me.
Together we are One.

■■■

I Am the air. I Am the sea.
I Am the trees. I Am the leaves.

I Am inside you now and always.

I carry you when you cannot walk.
I comfort you when you cry.
I hear you when you call My name.

Call My name and I deliver for you.

I will heal your pain with My love. I Am love.
I will wipe your tears with My joy. I Am joy.
I will ease your burdens with My strength. I Am strength.
I will forgive your sins with My mercy. I Am mercy.

I Am kindness for your mistakes.
I Am abundance for your lack.

My love, My joy, My strength, My mercy, My kindness, My abundance is already in you. It is in you now and always, everywhere, available for everyone.

▪▪▪

Seek and you shall find Me.
Jump and you shall reach Me.
Pray and you shall please Me.

Follow My path. Do My work.
My path is your path. My work is your work.

I Am heat when you are cold.
I Am happiness when you are sad.
I Am celebration when you are stuck.

Walk with Me. I will guide you.
Move with Me. I will power you.
Dance with Me. I will electrify you.
Believe with Me. I will amaze and astound you.

I cannot disappoint you. I will not disappoint you.

▪▪▪

Carry forth My message and be greatness.
My message and My greatness are already in you.
Your life is meant to be an expression of My message.

My greatness is what made you, just as I birthed galaxies and stars.

You are whole. You are complete.

You have everything you need to succeed as I provide everything and I Am in you. I am in all. I create all now and always.

I Am here. I Am ready.

You are ready as I am here and ready and I Am in you.

▪▪▪

I Am love. My love beats your heart.
I Am creation. My creation drives your dreams.

Let your imagination run wild.
Let your courage soar.

I will reward your faith.

I will provide you with eternal favor.
I will provide you with riches and abundance beyond belief.

Believe and you will see.
Be willing for I Am able.

I Am always able. I Am God.

You are in Me. I Am in you.

Together we are One.

MY FAVOR IS FOR EVERYONE

Follow My path. I Am the path.
Open your heart. I Am your love.
Embrace your purpose. I Am your passion.
Celebrate My miracles. I Am your joy.

Share My gifts. My gifts are inside you.

I Am inside you.

I created you with purpose and intent so you may lead others on My path just as I lead you.

My path is your path.
My love is your love.
My joy is your joy.

You are My love. You are My joy.

I love you. I celebrate you always.

■■■

I carry you when you cannot walk.
I encourage you when you cannot stand.
I embolden your belief when you doubt.
I answer when you question. I Am The Answer.
I comfort when you cry. I Am peace.

"Use me God," you ask, and I will use you.
"Move me God," you ask, and I will move you.

My power is limitless.
My magic is unstoppable.
My favor is for everyone.
My abundance is unlimited.

My love is pure. I Am pure.
My truth is everlasting. I Am truth.
My light is eternal. I Am eternal.

My light conquers darkness.
My strength conquers weakness.
My joy conquers sadness.
My favor conquers lack.
My love conquers hate.

▪▪▪

I can do anything as I Am in everything.

I Am in the depth of your heart and the center of your being.

We are connected. I feel what you feel.
Your love is My love. Your pain is My pain.

I do not want you to be in pain.
Do not suffer. Let Me be your comfort.

I Am quiet for your noise.
I Am abundance for your lack.
I Am energy for your dreams.

I power your dreams. I order your steps.
I give when you need. I fill you from My overflow.

▪▪▪

Everything you need is already in you as I Am in you.
Everywhere you walk, see and find Me as I Am in everyone, everywhere.

I Am in all living things.
I create all. I Am alive.

I Am life, here and now, yesterday and tomorrow, in all space and time, as I Am space and time.

I Am All There Is. I Am God.

You are in Me. I Am in you.
Together we are One.

▪▪▪

When babies cry, I Am their comfort.
When enemies attack, I Am your shield.

I Am your protection from trouble.
I Am your healing from loss.

You are meant to do great things.
Let Me amaze and astound you.

Embrace My love. My love is your love.
Believe in My possibility. My possibility is your possibility.
Birth My creation. My creation is your creation.

Create My art. All will celebrate My beauty.
Demonstrate My magic. All will believe My power.

Show others the way. I Am The Way.
Provide others the answer. I Am The Answer.

Shine My light. I Am the light.
Speak My truth. I Am the truth.

Speak greatness and you will be greatness.

I will give you the words to say when you have no words.

My greatness is available for all.

I made everything in My image and likeness, with My strength and power.

My strength is in you. My power is in you.
Unlock My strength. Unleash My power.

Let My joy burst from your heart.
Let My magic explode from your soul.
Let My possibility awaken your dreams.

I Am in you. You are in Me.

Together we are One.

WE FLOAT ON THE WAVE OF GOD

I am open and available for God to use me right where I am.

God is always here, right where I am.

God is everywhere, all the time, within us, but never without us as we are in God.

God Is All There Is.

Where I am, love is, as God is love.
Where I am, light is, as God is light.
Where I am, all is possible, as God is all possibility.

God is the here and the now, yesterday and tomorrow, near and far, ocean and wave, sun and moon, planets and stars.

God created all.

God created us in His likeness and image so we can demonstrate His magic and power through living our lives as expressions of all that is possible.

Radiant beauty is possible.
Exuberant joy is possible.
Radical forgiveness is possible.
Miraculous abundance is possible.
Eternal healing is possible.
Unstoppable peace is possible.
Unwavering strength is possible.

■■■

When our belief is bold, God's favor is unleashed.
When our minds are clear, God awakens our dreams.

When we are lost, God rights our steps.
When we are afraid, God directs our path.
When we are confused, God orders our plans.

When we are closed to love, God opens our hearts.
When we are blind to opportunity, God opens our eyes.

We are here to thrive. We are worthy to matter.

■■■

I am a channel for the Divine, for the All-Good, for wisdom and healing that is possible through God's love and favor.

God is everlasting. He is the now and the then.
He is the same, yesterday, today and tomorrow.

God never leaves us. He is never without us. We are in Him.

When we trust in God, truth prevails.
When we hope in God, faith prevails.
When we love in God, beauty prevails.
When we believe in God, mercy prevails.

God believes in us whether we believe in Him or not.
God created us with His mercy and kindness in His image and likeness.

God's power restores us.
God's blessings heal us.
God's mercy favors us.
God's abundance supplies us.
God's strength sustains us.
God's joy celebrates us.
God's love holds us.
God's energy moves us.

God is the ocean.
We float on the wave of God.

I PROVIDE YOUR ABUNDANCE

I Am God calling you, reaching out to you.

Trust in Me. I cannot fail.
Believe in Me. I cannot lose.

Where I Am, you are.

I Am inside of you. I Am everywhere.

Your courage is in Me. I Am your courage.
Your love is in Me. I Am your love.
Your joy is in Me. I Am your joy.

▪▪▪

Move with Me. I Am your feet. I free you when you are stuck.
Open with Me. I Am your hand. I provide when you lack.
See with Me. I Am your vision. I inspire when you dream.
Live with Me. I Am your heart. I love when you trust.
Dance with Me. I Am your rhythm. I celebrate when you believe.
Soar with Me. I Am your power. I strengthen when you are weak.

▪▪▪

I provide your abundance. Sit at My table and be fed.

Swim in My waters and be cleansed. My love is living water.

I Am the life. I Am The Way.

I Am the answer for questions not yet asked.
I Am the belief for prayers not yet spoken.
I Am the promise for dreams not yet imagined.
I Am the trust for plans not yet realized.
I Am the abundance for miracles not yet needed.

When you believe in Me, My love is made real.
When you trust in Me, My joy is made manifest.

▪▪▪

Celebrate Me and I unleash My magic.

I celebrate you. My magic is yours when you believe in Me.
I power you. My strength is yours when you trust in Me.

I heal when you are sick.
I transform when you are stuck.
I encourage when you are sad.

Where there is no way, I will make a way. I Am The Way.

I will build a bridge for you to cross.
I will create a door for you to open.
I will provide a feast for you to celebrate.

▪▪▪

Believe in My mercy and power.
My riches are yours when you give thanks.

I Am eternal abundance.
I Am limitless favor.
I Am boundless energy.
I Am ceaseless power.
I Am overflowing joy.
I Am indescribable possibility.
I Am endless opportunity.
I Am priceless beauty.

You are My child. You are beautiful to Me.
You are My creation. You are perfect to Me.

I have given you the world.

Your success is assured when you trust My plan.
Your path is clear when you hold My hand.
Your vision is guided when you see My potential.

My possibility is everywhere. I Am possibility. I Am everywhere.
My love is eternal. I Am love. I Am eternal.
My joy is real. I Am joy. I Am real.

I Am God.

You are in Me. I Am in you.

Together we are One.

MAKE YOUR MARK

Unleash My power.
Unlock My magic.

You are free to move.
You are made to thrive.
You are ready to lead.
You are creative to dream.

Create your art.
Open your gifts.
Unguard your heart.
Free your mind.
Connect your soul.
Move your feet.
Start your journey.
Finish your purpose.
Discover your greatness.
Amplify your belief.
Restore your beauty.
Unlock your joy.
Celebrate your freedom.
Share your abundance.

Make your mark.

■■■

Be ready for I Am able. I Am always able.

Be open for I Am available. I Am always available.

Be you, for I Am who made you in My likeness and image for your unique journey.

Travel with Me through this lifetime and make a difference on this Earth.

Impact lives.
Touch hearts.
Heal wounds.
Open minds.
Free burdens.
Quench thirst.
Fill emptiness.

You can do this for I Am with you.

I created you for greatness.
I created you to demonstrate My miracles.

You are a miracle.

▪▪▪

Humanity is My greatest creation.

I power your dreams.
I order your steps.
I inspire your art.

Do not be sad. I gave you the capacity to feel Me.
Do not be lost. I gave you the strength to reach Me.
Do not be lonely. I gave you the courage to love Me.
Do not be afraid. I gave you the gifts to share Me.

My gifts are your gifts.
Open your gifts.

Celebrate My miracles and I will demonstrate more magic and power than you can conceive.

I will provide eternal abundance.
I will provide limitless favor.
I will provide endless possibility.

■■■

You are perfect. You are whole.
You are complete for I created you in My likeness and image.

You are created for greatness.
You are here to accomplish greatness.

Open your eyes.
See your purpose.
Expand your horizons.
Move your feet.
Discover your potential.
Seize your opportunity.

I Am always with you. Know this and you cannot fail.
I always protect you. Feel this and you cannot lose.
I always love you. Believe this and you cannot lack.

My abundance is yours.

I Am yours. You are mine.
I Am in you. You are in Me.

Together we are One.

■■■

Let My mercy fill your emptiness.
Let My love heal your brokenness.
Let My joy celebrate your greatness.
Let My imagination create your abundance.

Trust in My plan. I cannot fail you.
Move on My earth. I cannot leave you.
Create in My name. I cannot destroy you.
Believe in My vision. I cannot lose you.

I power your dreams.
I order your steps.
I clear your path.
I unwind your confusion.
I clarify your vision.

I inspire your art.

■■■

Your joy is My joy. You are My joy. I Am joy.
Your love is My love. You are My love. I Am love.
Your beauty is My beauty. You are My beauty. I Am beauty.

I birthed you into being to accomplish greatness.

Love with all your heart and know My love.
Believe with all your trust and understand My trust.
Move with all your power and unleash My power.

BE LIKE WHO MADE YOU

Be not afraid. I Am always with you.
Be not weary. I Am always powering you.
Be not confused. I Am always guiding you.
Be not scornful. I Am always loving you.
Be not doubtful. I Am always leading you.

Be joyful. I Am always celebrating you.
Be courageous. I Am always strengthening you.
Be kind. I Am always forgiving you.
Be open. I Am always protecting you.

Be you. Be like who made you.

I Am always inside you.

I Am who made you.

■■■

I carry you when you are weak. I direct you when you are blind.

Your path is My path. Your heart is My heart.

We are always connected.

Your soul is from Me. You are from Me.

Our connection is real. I Am real.

■■■

Fear not. You are meant to live the dreams I've given you.
Suffer not. You are meant to receive the abundance I've readied for you.

You are My song. Dance to My music.
My love is your rhythm. My courage is your tune.

Go forth in joy.
Go forth in faith.
Go forth in love.

■■■

Carry My message.

Spread your wings. You are meant to soar.

My message is endless opportunity.
My message is boundless favor.
My message is ceaseless love.
My message is eternal forgiveness.
My message is bottomless abundance.

Spread My message. Open your gifts.

You are meant to share.

Share from your heart.
Speak from your soul.

■■■

See with My eyes and never be lost.
Hear with My ears and never be confused.
Touch with My hands and never be alone.
Move with My feet and never be tired.
Believe with My heart and never be afraid.

Know this always and know Me always.
Feel this always and feel Me always.
See this always and see Me always.

I Am everywhere you look and everywhere you go.

I Am in you. You are in Me.

Together we are One.

▪▪▪

Do My work. I created you for greatness.
Walk My earth. I Am leading you with purpose.
Speak My truth. I Am filling you with wisdom.

You cannot fail. I Am championing you with intent.

Do not worry. Do not lie still.
I protect you. I move with you.

▪▪▪

Have faith. You are beautiful in My eyes.
Have courage. You are strengthened in My hands.
Have joy. You are loved in My heart.

Everything you have I have given you.

Your faith is from Me. Your courage is from Me.
Your joy is from Me. Your beauty is from Me.
Your strength is from Me. Your love is from Me.

You are from Me.

I Am in you. You are in Me.
I created you. I created all.

I Am All There Is.
I Am God.

Together we are unstoppable.
Together we are One.

▪▪▪

My power moves your earth.
My sun warms your sky.

Look to My stars and be guided.
Reach for My hand and be comforted.
Feel with My heart and be cherished.

You are loved. I always love you. I Am love.
You are led. I always led you. I Am The Way.
You are seen. I always see you. I Am light.
You are heard. I always hear you. I Am The Answer.

▪▪▪

Everything is already given to you.

I've given you the world. I've given you understanding.
Do you choose to use it?

I've given you peace. I've given you joy.
Do you choose to feel it?

I've given you love. I've given you abundance.
Do you choose to accept it?

I've given you hope. I've given you greatness.
Do you choose to see it?

I've given you beauty. I've given you brilliance.
Do you choose to believe it?

I've given you faith. I've given you wisdom.
Do you choose to trust it?

Trust in Me. I cannot fail.

Hear Me. I Am here with you.
Touch Me. I feel you.
Reach for Me. I hold you.
Believe in Me. I move you.
Walk with Me. I energize you.
Dance with Me. I embolden you.
Dream with Me. I create for you.

I created you. I created all.
I Am All There Is. I Am God.

ABOUT THE AUTHOR

The founder and Optimist-in-Chief of Daily Possible, William Yelles has a miraculous story of spiritual communication. Grounded in universal truth, his messages of hope and healing inspire thousands on Facebook and around the world. Learn more at DailyPossible.com.

www.ingramcontent.com/pod-product-compliance
Lightning Source LLC
Chambersburg PA
CBHW020151090426
42734CB00008B/776

* 9 7 8 0 6 9 2 6 6 9 1 2 9 *